UNMASKING ADMINISTRATIVE EVIL

∩∩∩ Advances
||| || in Public
Administration

Sponsored by
the **Public Administration Theory Network**
and **College of Urban and Public Affairs
Portland State University**

Advances in Public Administration is a series of books designed both to encourage and to contribute to the vital processes of rethinking public administration and reconceptualizing various aspects of the field in an insightful manner that goes well beyond traditional approaches.

UNMASKING
ADMINISTRATIVE
E   V   I   L

GUY B. ADAMS
DANNY L. BALFOUR

SAGE Publications
International Educational and Professional Publisher
Thousand Oaks London New Delhi

For information:

SAGE Publications, Inc.
2455 Teller Road
Thousand Oaks, California 91320
E-mail: order@sagepub.com

SAGE Publications Ltd.
6 Bonhill Street
London EC2A 4PU
United Kingdom

SAGE Publications India Pvt. Ltd.
M-32 Market
Greater Kailash I
New Delhi 110 048 India

Printed in the United States of America

Library of Congress Cataloging-in-Publication Data

Adams, Guy B.
 Unmasking administrative evil / by Guy B. Adams and Danny L. Balfour.
  p. cm. -- (Advances in public administration)
  Includes bibliographical references and index.
  ISBN 0-7619-0668-1 (acid-free paper)
  ISBN 0-7619-0669-X (pbk. : acid-free paper)
  1. Public administration--Moral and ethical aspects. I. Balfour,
  Danny L. II. Title. III. Series.
 JF1525.E8 A33 1998
 351--ddc21   98-8931

This book is printed on acid-free paper.
   99   00   01   02   03   04   10   9   8   7   6   5   4   3   2

Acquisition Editor:	Catherine Rossbach
Editorial Assistant:	Heidi van Middlesworth
Production Editor:	Wendy Westgate
Production Assistant:	Denise Santoyo
Typesetter/Designer:	Rose Tylak
Cover Designer:	Ravi Balasuriya
Print Buyer:	Anna Chin

Contents

Series Editor's Introduction

Few eras have seen so much evil and yet effectively distanced themselves from that evil as has our own. Whether this dissociation has been intentional or a byproduct of 20th-century life I will leave to others, but it is arguably a pervasive characteristic of our time.

This distancing has been accomplished in a number of ways. To begin with, we have often placed ethical values beyond the realm of useful discussion, particularly in the social sciences. Then, we have frequently severed the intimate connection between our intentional actions and our responsibility for them. Last, we have tended to portray guilt and shame, those consummate pricks to conscience, as corrosive to the psyche or impossible to support in a diverse society.

One need not go far to find examples. The logical positivist empiricism that has dominated the temper of the social sciences through much of the 20th century has placed ethical concepts in the realm of a "non-sense," relegating them to little more than matters of personal taste, well beyond the possibility of fruitful reason and reflection (MacIntyre, 1981).

At the same time, the alchemy of the marketplace tends to transmute self-interest, no matter how ill intentioned, into the gold of general welfare. The technocratic separation of means and ends and the workings of bureaucratic specialization have further obscured the moral relationship between what humans do and the effect these actions have on others (Hummel, 1987). Last, guilt and shame, the sentinels of evil, have become marginalized in both psychology and sociology. Popular versions of Freudianism have chosen to view guilt as individually dysfunctional and incapacitating. Its social counterpart, shame, has fared little better, as our society loses the traditional solidarity on which shame relies as a social control mechanism. As a result, both guilt and shame have become terms to avoid as we become more reluctant to use evil's name even where it is palpably present.

With the marginalization of evil has come its trivialization by the media. Enormities become nightly fare for the "home theater" where real and fictional horrors often seem to meld into one another. As a result, a paradoxical situation arises in which we become hardened to the evils of our time while we remain strangely reluctant to call evil, to its face, that which is in fact evil.

At century's end, determined voices are rising around us, calling us to face the evils of past and present and to give them names, identities, and, most important, lucid explanations. The authors of this book can be counted among this number. Adams and Balfour set themselves the task of unmasking administrative evil, and in doing so, they give themselves the job of examining what in a real sense is the paradigm case of evil in the 20th century—evil as it arises and works its way behind the bland, amoral facade of technocracy and the administrative state. Let no reader make the mistake of assuming this volume is "just about public administration." It is about all of us and how we have faced, or failed to face, real wickedness when we have encountered it in our lives.

—Henry D. Kass
Coordinating Editor
Advances in Public Administration

Foreword

In 1961, for a series of articles Hannah Arendt was going to write for *The New Yorker*, she traveled to Jerusalem to attend the trial proceedings of the notorious war criminal Adolf Eichmann. As she sat in the back of the courtroom taking copious notes, she heard Eichmann, among other things, repeatedly claim that he was in many ways actually sickened by some of the mass murdering he witnessed in the concentration camps. He went on to reiterate, with almost an eerie calmness to his voice as he stood within his bulletproof glass cage, that he had nothing personal against the Jews (or anybody else for that matter), even as, in his next breath, he admitted that with meticulous care he organized the deportation of hundreds of thousands of people to their deaths. Moreover, Eichmann claimed that as much as some of the camps he visited were (at times) repugnant to him, he never let those feelings—at any time— interfere with his more important role in performing the administrative duties consistent with the goals and purposes of the Third Reich.

Ironically, Eichmann tried to invoke nothing other than Immanuel Kant's categorical imperative to justify his behavior: If he had disobeyed these administrative orders, then every soldier (from any army) would have the right, if not the obligation, to disobey any order found to be personally objectionable. It was an argument, as Arendt has pointed out, deeply ingrained in the subversion of language and the atrophy of thought itself—an instrumental perspective that found its most frightening expression in administrative language that attempted to mask the conduct of Nazi administrative operations: mass killings replaced by the new word "evacuation" or deportation by the new phrases of "resettlement" and "labor in the East." The argument also reflected Eichmann's mechanical thoughtlessness as well as his inability to exhibit any independent critical thinking. Eichmann's "banality of evil" (as Arendt called it) even today is an unsettling dimension of public affairs. Even as he was going to be hanged for his crimes against humanity, he remained captive to this thoughtlessness, thanking his beloved homeland, Austria; praising Germany as a country he tried to serve so well; and finally thanking Argentina for giving him a place to hide until he was captured by Israeli agents. He voiced how he would never forget them. No thought—even in his last words—was ever expressed to those he had played such a major role in systematically murdering.

Many aspects of Arendt's controversial argument concerning Eichmann need not concern us here. What is salient about Arendt's basic argument, particularly in the light of Guy Adams and Danny Balfour's important new book about administrative evil, is that Eichmann represented a new kind of evildoer whose evil was accomplished within and conforming to acceptable organizational roles and policies. According to their analysis, the Holocaust was (obviously) a clear instance of administrative evil, an evil unmasked. At times, administrative *evil* (a word rarely referred to in the fields of public administration and public policy) can be more subtle and opaque. At this point, they explain, administrative evil becomes masked. Herein lies, I think, Adams and Balfour's important contribution to public ethics. They anchor their argument within the broader milieu of technical rationality—a rationality that essentially has stripped reason of any normative role in shaping human affairs. Specifically, in regard to public administration and public policy, they trace how technical rationality has, to a large degree, determined the boundaries of these respective fields, starting in the Progressive Era of a century ago.

As they argue, this analytical-technical mind-set does not offer enough of a bulwark against what they refer to as "moral inversion"; that is, an invitation to administrative evil that can come in the form of an expert or technical role working on what supposedly is a good and worthy project. What is particularly troubling to Adams and Balfour is that public service ethics and professional ethics are, by and large, both embedded in a technical-rational approach to public affairs. As they assert in Chapter 1, "because administrative evil wears many masks, it is entirely possible to adhere to the tenets of public service ethics and participate in a great evil, and not be aware of it until it is too late (or perhaps not at all)."

Within this context, they discuss the Marshall Space Flight Center and how the von Braun team of scientists came to the United States, even though close to 20,000 individuals died at Mittelbau-Dora in less than 2 years. Concomitantly, they posit the serious normative implications of a defensive organizational culture that developed at the Marshall Space Flight Center and explain how, almost inevitably, it set in motion a destructive culture that, to some degree, contributed to the space shuttle *Challenger* disaster. As polemic as this argument may seem, they proceed to address some major policy programs and how they represent disturbing reminders concerning the role of public administration in possessing a capacity for administrative evil. If nothing else, this part of their argument will provoke a debate, long overdue, concerning the nature and scope of administrative evil as part of public administration and public policy.

The challenge confronting us, Adams and Balfour maintain, is how we can unmask administrative evil, which will imply a fundamental rethinking of public administration's fixation on technical rationality. It will mean, at a minimum, fostering a critical view of public (and private) organizations and the instrumental-technical culture in which they are embedded. Although, it is true, they offer no definitive way of overcoming administrative evil, they do indicate that by developing a historical consciousness and a "public ethics" we can at least resist the more tempting moral inversions that are often clothed in managerial and analytical approaches.

I know—given the controversial nature of this book—that many will disagree with certain aspects of the arguments posed by the authors. I suspect many will also find themselves getting somewhat defensive about the broader implications of the book's lucid analysis. Whatever the reaction, we have here a book that will compel us to look at administrative evil in a way that we can no longer ignore. Perhaps, as we try to comprehend how administrative evil can take place and construe the different and subtle forms in which it can manifest itself, we might in fact be taking the first step in increasing our ability to resist it in whatever forms, or behind whatever masks, it tries to hide itself. In the end, Adams and Balfour echo a point made by Arendt (1958, p. viii) that is worth pondering: "Comprehension does not mean denying the outrageous, deducing the unprecedented from precedents, or explaining phenomena by such analogies and generalities that the impact of reality and the shock of experience are no longer felt. It means, rather, examining and bearing consciously the burden which our century has placed on us—neither denying its existence nor submitting meekly to its weight. Comprehension, in short, means the unpremeditated, attentive facing up to, and resisting of, reality—whatever it may be."

—Curtis Ventriss
University of Vermont

Acknowledgments

◆ The authors of this book first met at the 1993 meeting of the Public Administration Theory Network and only discovered nearly 2 years later that we had a common interest in the Holocaust and its implications for public administration. As academics, we have both read many books. Some have had a lasting and profound impact. Few have affected us more, and changed as significantly our outlook on the world and on our chosen field of study, than *The Cunning of History: The Holocaust and the American Future*, by Richard L. Rubenstein (1975). Although not written expressly about public administration, the book showed us that the Holocaust was an important, perhaps the most important, historical event in the history of our field, although it is in no way recognized as such by most other scholars and practitioners. Both of us continue to teach this book to MPA students; one of us has done so for 20 years.

Rubenstein's book opened up a new, and disturbing, perspective on public administration (and all professions in public life), a perspective that does not allow us to be satisfied with conventional understandings of the field in general, and of administrative ethics in particular. To a considerable extent, our book represents an attempt to deal with the profound issues raised by Rubenstein (and now a number of other scholars), and to suggest new directions for public administration that take into account a fuller history of the field and the reality of administrative evil. We both value and respect public administration and are ardent defenders of the good that our field and other professions can and do accomplish. At the same time, we believe that the future of public administration is imperiled by the field's lack of historical consciousness and attendant blindness to the potential for administrative evil to erupt in our midst.

Researching and writing *Unmasking Administrative Evil* has been a valuable learning experience for both authors. This is due in large measure to the many friends and colleagues who have helped us throughout the process. Professor Henry Kass of Portland State University, the editor of the Sage Series on Advances in Public Administration, has been a strong supporter of this project from the beginning. Catherine Rossbach, public administration editor par excellence for Sage Publications, believed in this book at the beginning and provided support that made a difference along the way. Professor Curtis Ventriss of the University of Vermont served as the series reviewer for this volume and, in addition to providing his perceptive comments, has written the foreword for this book. Professor Bayard Catron of George Washington University and Dr. Stuart Gilman of the U.S. Office of Government Ethics read the book in draft form and provided especially useful comments. Professors Ralph Hummel, Cynthia McSwain, and Dvora Yanow provided useful commentary when the book was at the proposal stage.

We appreciate the expert assistance of several individuals. Dr. Michael Neufeld, curator at the National Air and Space Museum in Washington, D.C., was very generous with his time and offered useful advice in dealing with the history of the von Braun team of rocket scientists and engineers. From a different perspective, Dr. Steven Luckert of the U.S.

Holocaust Memorial Museum and Eli Rosenbaum, director of the Office of Special Investigations in the U.S. Department of Justice, were also helpful in this same area. Roger Boisjoly read the entire manuscript and provided useful technical assistance on space shuttle issues.

Guy Adams would like to thank his colleagues at the University of Missouri-Columbia, particularly Professor Michael Diamond, who read each and every draft of the book. Professor Lee Wilkins and Seth Allcorn also read the book in draft form and offered useful feedback, as did Susan Eckerle, an MPA student. Cam Stivers and Richard Box have been important intellectual companions along this path of inquiry. Dean Bruce Walker of the College of Business and Public Administration has consistently provided intellectual encouragement. My family, Martha, Kate, and Dave, not only gave their special kind of support and encouragement but also provided the best possible antidote to dwelling so much on the topic of evil.

Danny Balfour would like to thank his colleagues at the University of Akron and at Grand Valley State University. Special thanks go to Frank Marini for his support and guidance in the early stages of this project, and to William Baum for his insights into the Holocaust and for access to his great library. Others who were willing to listen and thus made this a better book include Dean Nancy Harper, Beth Kinsley Warner, Charles Fox, Hugh Miller, and Cheryl Simrell King. Finally, special appreciation is due to my wife, Mayumi, and son, Trevor, who help to keep all things in proper perspective.

—Guy B. Adams
—Danny L. Balfour

Cruelty and compassion come with the chromosomes;
All men are merciful and all are murderers.
Doting on dogs, they build their Dachaus;
Fire whole cities and fondle the orphans;
Are loud against lynching, but all for Oakridge;
Full of future philanthropy, but today the NKVD.
Whom shall we persecute, for whom feel pity?
It is all a matter of the moment's mores,
Of words on wood pulp, of radios roaring,
Of Communist kindergartens and first communions.
Only in the knowledge of his own Essence
Has any man ceased to be many monkeys.

                                   (Huxley, 1948, p. 75.)

Introduction and Overview

A Century of Progress
                    —title of the 1933 Chicago World's Fair

Science Explores, Technology Executes, Mankind Conforms
                              —motto of the 1933 World's Fair

◈ We begin with the premise that evil is inherent in the human condition. As one examines the sweep of human history, clearly there have been many great and good deeds and achievements, as well as real progress in the quality of at least many humans' lives. We also see century after century of mind-numbing, human-initiated violence, betrayal, and tragedy. Those instances in which humans knowingly and deliberately inflict pain and suffering on other human beings, we call *evil*. In Chapter 1, we offer a more ample characterization of evil; however, evil is one of those phenomena in human life that defy easy definition and understanding.

Those readers who can look at human history and see no evil may find little interest in this book. Others who acknowledge negative interaction in human affairs but prefer more modern terminology, for example, "dysfunctional behavior," may find our use of a very old word, "evil," uncomfortable or even misguided. We ask that these readers set aside their objections and give the argument a chance to convince them. Still others may readily acknowledge evil in human affairs and find our argument—that evil appears in a new and dangerous form in the modern age—fairly easy to follow.

The modern age, especially in the last hundred years, has had as its hallmark what we call *technical rationality*. Technical rationality is a way of thinking and living (a culture) that emphasizes the scientific-analytic mind-set and the belief in technological progress. Chapter 2 explains this notion and its historical evolution at considerable length. For our purposes here, the culture of technical rationality also has introduced a new and frightening form of evil that we call *administrative evil*. What is different about administrative evil, as our title implies, is that its appearance is *masked*. Administrative evil may be masked in many different ways, but the common characteristic is that people can engage in acts of evil without being aware that they are in fact doing anything at all wrong. Indeed, ordinary people may simply be acting appropriately in their organizational role—in essence, just doing what those around them would agree they should be doing—and at same time be participating in what a critical and reasonable observer, usually well after the fact, would call evil. Even worse, under conditions of what we call *moral inversion*, in which something evil has been redefined convincingly as good, ordinary people can all too easily engage in acts of administrative evil while believing that what they are doing is not only correct but, in fact, good.

The basic difference between evil as it has appeared throughout human history and administrative evil, which is a fundamentally modern phenomenon, is that the latter is less easily seen. People have always been able to delude themselves into thinking that their evil acts are not really so bad, and we have certainly had moral inversions in times past, but there are three very important differences in administrative evil. One is our modern inclination to *unname* evil, an old concept that does not lend itself well to the scientific-analytic mind-set. The second difference is the modern, complex organization, which diffuses individual responsibility and requires the compartmentalized accomplishment of role expectations to perform work on a daily basis. The third difference is the way in which the culture of technical rationality has analytically narrowed the processes by which public policy is formulated and implemented, so that moral inversions are now more likely. Our goal in this book is to illuminate at least some of the dynamics in organizations and in public policy that mask administrative evil.

Earlier, we noted that evil involves the knowing and deliberate inflicting of pain and suffering on others. If administrative evil essentially means that people inflict pain and suffering on others, but do so *not* knowingly or deliberately, are these actions still evil? In other words, ordinary people may indeed inflict pain and suffering on others, but they do so in the course of performing their organizational or policy role appropriately. They were just following orders and just doing their job. What this means is that identifying administrative evil is difficult and fraught with possibilities for missing it altogether, or perhaps worse, calling mistakes or misjudgments evil. We argue here that identifying administrative evil becomes more difficult especially within one's own culture and in one's own historical time period. Conversely, identifying administrative evil is easier if it occurred in another culture or country and if it occurred in the past.

Our discussion of administrative evil begins with the Holocaust of World War II. Here we refer to administrative evil as unmasked, and we suggest that identifying administrative evil is easier because the Holocaust was perpetrated by Germans (and others complicit with them) and because it occurred more than 50 years ago. Although the evil—the pain and suffering unto death—that was inflicted on millions of "others" in the Holocaust (Glass, 1997) was so horrific as to almost defy our comprehension, it was also clearly an instance of administrative evil. The Holocaust occurred in modern times in a culture suffused with technical rationality, and most of its activity was accomplished within organizational roles and within accepted public policy. Although the results of the Holocaust were horrific and arguably without precedent in human history, ordinary Germans fulfilling ordinary roles carried out this incredible destruction in ways that had been successfully packaged as socially normal and appropriate (Arendt, 1963). Nothing else in human history really compares with this event, and certainly all else in modern times pales before its example. We are concerned to point out most emphatically that we do not "compare" in any way our American examples of administrative evil with the Holocaust.

The Holocaust, which occurred in another culture and more than a half century ago, was discussed and studied very little in the United States for 25 years after the fact. As we move in Chapters 4-6 progressively to examples and discussions that occurred within our own culture and closer to our own time, the dynamics of administrative evil become progressively more subtle and opaque. Here we refer to administrative evil as masked. This is one of the central points of our argument: Administrative evil is not easily identified as such because its appearance is masked; moreover, in our ordinary roles with our taken for granted assumptions about the modern world, *we wear the mask.*

Dirty Hands

Machiavelli (c. 1520/1961), in *The Prince*, still offers perhaps the clearest expression of the *dirty hands* conundrum in political action and public life. In public life, we have always had to deal with questions of conscience that arise when one chooses what one hopes is a small evil as a means of achieving a greater good on behalf of others. *Raisons d'état,* or reasons of state, are advanced as good and valid reasons for engaging in minor, and sometimes not so minor, acts of evil. The problem of dirty hands has always had within it a subtle temptation, which has at times led to great evil in human history. Jean-Paul Sartre (1948), the French existential philosopher, wrote a play, *Les Mains Sales* (Dirty Hands), precisely on this subject. One author has described the play as

> a fatalistic mockery of the bold adventurer in politics who feels fit to decide for others as though the future were a game of chess in an empty room; the play insists that one cannot predict what will happen as a result of one's act, from the basis of what one might want to think one had intended to happen. (Sutherland, 1995, p. 490)

The arrogant flaw of dirty hands, however, is different altogether from administrative evil.

The dirty hands choice means that one inflicts on others, knowingly and deliberately, pain and suffering (limited, one hopes, to the minimum) *for a good reason*—for the greater good of the polity. Whether and when such a choice is justified has been widely debated, but it does not bear significantly on the topic of this book. Administrative evil is different in part because the culture of technical rationality tends to drive the consideration of ethics out of the picture altogether, much less the rational calculation of how much good legitimately can be traded off against evil. Because administrative evil is masked, we typically do not see ethics in the situation at all, which means that we do not even see a choice about which we might calculate degrees of good.

Hubris

Hubris is another very old word, referring to an inflated pride or sense of self—a phenomenon seen often in connection with "dirty hands," as just discussed. Hubris is not a necessary component of administrative evil, but when combined, they represent a particularly deadly combination. Although not discussed in great depth here, the career of Albert Speer, Hitler's minister of armaments, shows with remarkable clarity how hubris and administrative evil can combine with terrible results (Speer, 1970; see also Sereny, 1995). Wernher von Braun, whose career is treated in some detail in Chapters 4 and 5, was also marked by hubris, as was Robert McNamara (Saul, 1992), whose career we briefly discuss in Chapter 6. Hubris might be compared to an accelerant that, when added to an existing fire (administrative evil), can easily escalate something seemingly small into a conflagration.

One other point needs to be made. Although our own academic home is public administration and the arguments and examples in the book are overwhelmingly from the public sector, we believe the arguments hold for all professions and disciplines involved in public affairs or in public life most generally. Further, we believe a similar argument about administrative evil could be made from the perspective of the private sector. An obvious starting point could be the American tobacco industry. We are convinced that administrative evil is a phenomenon of the culture of technical rationality and as such is certainly not confined to the public sector.

Overview of the Book

In Chapter 1, "The Dynamics of Evil and Administrative Evil," we attempt to provide a richer and deeper characterization of evil in general and of administrative evil in particular. The connection between evil and public administration (and other related fields and professions) is discussed, as is the failure to recognize instances of administrative evil. In an attempt to better understand evil itself, we provide a framework based on the insights of object-relations psychology. We also examine the role of perspective and distance, and of language and dehumanization, in the dynamics of evil. Next, a social constructionist perspective is used in an attempt to understand the apparent ease with which people participate in acts of administrative evil, and the role of social compliance in this dynamic. Finally, we show how individual, organizational, and social behaviors interact in ways that can lead to administrative evil. This chapter strives to lay the foundation for understanding the examples of administrative evil discussed in subsequent chapters.

A central theme of the modern age is the emphasis on the value of technical rationality and the attendant narrowing of the concepts of reason, professionalism, ethics, and politics. When linked to bureaucracy and organization, the result is an unintentional tendency toward dehumanization and the elevation of technical progress and processes over human values and dignity. Recent advances in the development of the digital computer and information systems are as likely to exacerbate these tendencies as to empower or liberate. In Chapter 2, "The Framework of Administrative Evil: Modernity and Technical Rationality," we show how modern public administration has its roots in the Progressive Era of a century ago, as do many other fields and professions. We argue that the parameters of the field, defined largely by technical rationality, were effectively set during this period and have not deviated appreciably since then. Eruptions of evil in the 20th century, such as the Holocaust and its organization and management, spring from these same historical antecedents, albeit in a different society. This framework, we suggest, has enabled a new and frightening form of evil—administrative evil.

Chapter 3, "Administrative Evil Unmasked: The Holocaust and Public Administration," reviews interpretations of the Holocaust with a primary focus on its management and administration. Here we show how the combination of state power and authority and advances in modern, technical-rational administrative practice were central to the implementation of this paradigmatic case of administrative evil. In fact, the existence of an advanced, public administration infrastructure allowed the Nazis to surpass all others in the magnitude and efficiency of their killing. Public administration, in the form of ordinary civil servants carrying out legally sanctioned and routine bureaucratic processes, played a key role in all parts of the Holocaust, including the composition and management of the civil service, the compiling of lists and management of files, defining the legal status of victims and their property, the organization of ghetto communities, transportation management, the administration of death/slave labor camps, and the coordination of all these and other activities. In short, the Holocaust was a massive administrative undertaking, which leads us to consider whether modern public administration may be at its most effective and efficient operating levels when engaging in programs of dehumanization and destruction—even if the very thought is repugnant.

Chapter 4, "Administrative Evil Masked: From Mittelbau-Dora and Peenemünde to the Marshall Space Flight Center," reviews a case in which we begin to see the increasing difficulty of identifying clear instances of administrative evil within our own culture and within our own time. Here we show how the instrumental aim of attaining technical superiority over all others resulted in American military intelligence officers and other public servants crossing legal and moral boundaries to bring the von Braun team of German rocket scientists and engineers to our country after World War II. We discuss the roles played by Wernher von Braun and several other team members in proposing and then making extensive use of SS-provided slave labor to construct V-2 rockets as part of the Third Reich's war effort. First at Peenemünde, the Nazi rocket development and production facility, then at Mittelbau-Dora, the last of the SS concentration camps and the only one devoted solely to weapons production, some of the von Braun team members, including Wernher von Braun himself, engaged in activities for which others were convicted of war crimes in postwar Germany.

Brought to the United States under Operations Overcast and Paperclip, their past was ignored, misrepresented, and then kept hidden as the von Braun team went on to play a key role in American space exploration at the Marshall Space Flight Center, including building the Saturn rockets that launched Apollo to the moon. The handful of these Germans, whose past was sullied by their actions in the Nazi Third Reich, had highly successful careers as executives in both the public and private sectors, suggesting that the specialized skills of managing in a technical-rational context transferred readily from the Third Reich to the postwar United States. Although it is true that such questions are more easily raised in hindsight, we ask whether the price for these achievements was too high—20,000 dead in less that 2 years at Mittelbau-Dora, with American public servants simply unconcerned about the direct participation of von Braun and a few others in the decisions and actions leading to those deaths, because their technical expertise was so desirable.

Chapter 5, "Organizational Dynamics and Administrative Evil: The Marshall Space Flight Center, NASA, and the Space Shuttle *Challenger*," shows how less visible dynamics of organizational culture can lead to administrative evil. We view the case of Marshall, NASA (National Aeronautics and Space Administration), and the space shuttle *Challenger* as an opaque and complex case in which the identification of administrative evil is problematic. We focus on the role of the Marshall Space Flight Center not only in the *Challenger* disaster but also, more significantly, within the overall space program. A defensive organizational culture, created by the von Braun team as a natural response to their feelings of isolation and of being slighted and even attacked by outsiders within NASA and in society at large, turned destructive under the leadership of Dr. William Lucas in the 1970s and 1980s. Even if the *Challenger* launch could have somehow been stopped, Marshall's destructive organizational culture, which ensured that critical information was either blocked or not acted on, placed the lives of astronauts in the space shuttle program needlessly at much greater than "normal" risk.

Chapter 6, "Public Policy and Administrative Evil," explores the implications of "problem solving" as a metaphor for how public policy is formulated and implemented, with a focus on the messy and intractable policy problems that may involve "surplus populations" (Rubenstein, 1975, 1983) and the potential for public policies of destruction based on moral inversions. What is especially problematic is the extent to which technical-rational problem solving has attained an unquestioned (and unspoken) dominance in the policy arena with little or no reflection on the possible destructive consequences of addressing social problems in this way. In the United States, many social problems persist, in part, because we choose to maintain what Berlin (1991) terms an "uneasy equilibrium" between competing values rather than pursue final, and potentially inhuman, solutions to social problems. In other words, the drive or desire to solve social problems such as poverty, crime, drug abuse, and illegal immigration has been balanced with concern for protecting political and human rights.

This equilibrium is threatened when the problem to be solved involves surplus populations. When the objects of public policy programs are considered expendable, or rendered "socially dead" (Goldhagen, 1996) and portrayed as unwanted vermin, or as a blight on society (Bauman, 1989), such moral inversions lead toward policies of destruction and elimination. There are many examples in American history of these destructive tendencies and policies. The decimation of Native American populations from the earliest days of colonization, the expropriation of property and forced internment of Japanese Americans in concentration camps during World War II, the Tuskegee and other exploitative experiments, and Operations Overcast and Paperclip are all disturbing reminders that American public administration also possesses a well-developed capacity for administrative evil. That we have so far fallen short of the scale and scope of the Holocaust should provide scant comfort.

Chapter 7, "In the Face of Administrative Evil: Finding a Basis for Ethics in the Public Service," does not provide a definitive direction or set of recommendations on how to avoid administrative evil in the future. The profound challenges that evil presents are such that it would be presumptuous to propose that we have any authoritative answers to them. At the same time, we do not want to suggest that public administration, as well as other fields and professions, is caught in a sort of Sartrean "no exit." We do believe that the unmasking of administrative evil means a sharp departure from the modern, technical-rational conception of public administration. Nor do we take a crisis of legitimacy for public administration as the core issue for the field. Efficient and legitimate institutions can be used for constructive or destructive purposes. The fundamental problem for public administration, given the ubiquity of administrative evil, is not to establish its institutional or academic legitimacy; rather, it is to develop and nurture a critical, reflexive attitude toward public institutions, the exercise of authority, and the culture at large. As difficult as this may be to imagine, much less to accomplish, even this offers no final guarantee against administrative evil.

Responsibility for the prevention of future acts of administrative evil rests, in part, with public administration theorists and practitioners (along with those in related professions and fields) who understand their role and identity in such a way that they can resist seductive and cunning temptations within moral inversions to apply expedient or ideological solutions to the many difficult issues that confront contemporary governance. In this view, public administration certainly encompasses, but is not centered on, the use of sophisticated organizational and management techniques in the implementation of public policy. Public administration must also, and primarily, be informed by a historical consciousness that is aware of the fearsome potential for evil on the part of the state and its agents, and by a societal role and identity infused not only with personal and professional ethics but also with a social and political

consciousness—a public ethics—that can recognize
the masks of administrative evil and refuse to act as its
accomplice.

The Dynamics of Evil and Administrative Evil

The effects which follow too constant and intense a concentration upon evil are always disastrous. Those who
crusade not for God in themselves, but against the devil
in others, never succeed in making the world better, but
leave it either as it was, or sometimes even perceptibly
worse than it was, before the crusade began. By thinking
primarily of evil we tend, however excellent our intentions, to create occasions for evil to manifest itself.
                              —*Aldous Huxley (1952, p. 192)*

Evil is not an accepted entry in the lexicon of the social
sciences. Social scientists much prefer to *describe* behavior, avoiding ethically loaded or judgmental rubrics—to
say nothing of what is normally considered religious phra-
seology. Evil nevertheless reverberates down through the
centuries of human history, showing little sign of weakening
at the dawn of the 21st century and the apex of modernity
(Lang, 1991). In the modern age, we are greatly enamored of
the notion of progress, of the belief that civilization is devel-
opmental, with the present age at the pinnacle of human

achievement. These beliefs constrain us from acknowl-
edging the implications of the fact that the 20th century has
been the bloodiest, both in absolute and relative terms, in
human history, and that we have developed the capacity for
even greater mass destruction.

Well more than a hundred million human beings have
been slaughtered or otherwise killed as a direct or indirect
consequence of the epidemic of wars and state-sponsored
violence in this century (Bauman, 1989; Eliot, 1972). Administrative mass murder and genocide have become a demonstrated capacity within the human social repertoire
(Rubenstein, 1975, 1983), and simply because such events
have occurred, new instances of genocide and dehumanization become more likely (Arendt, 1963). If we are to have any
realistic hope for ameliorating this trajectory in the coming
century, administrative evil needs to be unmasked and better
understood, especially by those likely to be a necessary
component in any future acts of mass destruction—public
administrators, as well as all other professionals and fields
active in public affairs.

Evil is defined in the *Oxford English Dictionary* as the
antithesis of good in all its principal senses. A more useful
behavioral definition of evil has been provided by Katz:

> Behavior that deprives innocent people of their humanity,
> from small scale assaults on a person's dignity to outright
> murder . . . [this definition] focuses on how people behave
> toward one another—where the behavior of one person, or
> an aggregate of persons is destructive to others. (1993, p. 5)

This behavioral definition suggests a continuum, with hor-
rible, mass eruptions of evil, such as the Holocaust and other,
lesser instances of mass murder, at one extreme, and the
"small" white lie, which is somewhat hurtful, at the other.
Certainly, at the white lie end of the continuum, use of the
term *evil* may stretch our credulity, although Sissela Bok

(1978) has argued persuasively that even so-called white lies can have serious personal and social consequences, especially as they accrue over time. For the most part, we discuss the end of the continuum where the recognition of evil may be easier and more obvious (at least when it is unmasked). The small-scale end of the continuum, however, remains of importance because the road to great evil often begins with seemingly small, first steps. Evil, in many cases, is enmeshed in cunning and seductive processes that can lead ordinary people in ordinary times down the proverbial slippery slope.

Where does evil come from and why does it persist? Thousands of years of human religious history have provided ample commentary on evil, and philosophers certainly have discussed it at length (Adams & Merrihew, 1990; Kateb, 1983; Katz, 1988; Kekes, 1990; Parkin, 1985; Russell, 1988; Sanford, 1981; Stein, 1997; Stivers, 1982; Twitchell, 1985). Although there was a time when locating evil in the symbolic persona of the devil provided adequate explanation of its origins, the modern scientific era both demands a more comprehensive explanation of the origins of evil and makes it nearly impossible to provide one. One author has argued that the modern age has been engaged in a process of unnaming evil, such that we now have a "crisis of incompetence" in facing evil (Delbanco, 1995, p. 3): "A gulf has opened up in our [modern] culture between the visibility of evil and the intellectual resources available for coping with it." Evil may not yet have become unnameable, although in its administrative manifestations it often goes unseen. Evil reveals itself to us depending on our approach and stance toward it, and in the modern age, the great risk is not seeing it at all, for administrative evil wears many masks.

Based on the premise that evil is inherent in the human condition, we make several key arguments in this book (which we introduced in the "Introduction and Overview"):

1. The modern age, with its scientific-analytic mind-set and technical-rational approach to social and political problems, enables a new and frightening form of evil—administrative evil. It is frightening because it wears many masks, making it easy for ordinary people to do evil, even when they do not intend to do so.

2. Because administrative evil wears a mask, no one has to accept an overt invitation to commit an evil act, because such overt invitations are very rarely issued. Rather, the invitation may come in the form of an expert or technical role, couched in the appropriate language, or it may even come packaged as a good and worthy project, representing what we call a *moral inversion*, in which something evil or destructive has been redefined as good and worthy.

3. We examine closely two of administrative evil's most favored masks. First, within modern organizations (both public and private), because so much of what occurs is *underneath* our awareness of it, we find people engaged in patterns and activities that may culminate in evil without their even being aware of it until after the fact (and often, not even then). Second, we look at social and public policies that can culminate in evil. These most often involve either an instrumental or a technical goal (which drives out ethics) or a *moral inversion* that is unseen by those pursuing such a policy.

4. Because public service ethics and professional ethics more generally are anchored in the scientific-analytic mind-set, in a technical-rational approach to administrative or social problems, and in the professions themselves, both are effectively useless in the face of administrative evil. Because administrative evil wears many masks, it is entirely possible to adhere to the tenets of public service ethics and participate in a great evil, and not be aware of it until it is too late (or perhaps not at all). Thus, finding a basis for public service ethics in the face of administrative evil is problematic at best.

Administrative Evil
and Public Administration

This book discusses the relationship between evil and public administration—a relationship that is usually overlooked or dismissed as involving temporary, politically induced departures from ethical standards, which themselves are founded on the presumed inherent neutrality or benevolence of rational administration (Frederickson & Hart, 1985). Although we address public administration directly, we believe the arguments presented here hold for all professions and for practitioners of all kinds whose activities are within public life in its most general sense. In this book, we argue and present evidence that the tendency toward administrative evil, as manifested primarily in acts of dehumanization and genocide, is deeply woven into the identity of public administration (and also into other fields and professions in public life). The influence of evil has been suppressed and masked despite, or perhaps because of, its profound and far-reaching implications for the future of public administration.

Despite what may initially seem to be a negative treatment of the public service, it is not our intention to somehow diminish public administration, engage in bureaucrat bashing, or give credence to misguided arguments that governments and their agents are necessarily or inherently evil. In fact, our aim is quite the opposite: to get beyond the superficial critiques and lay the groundwork for a more ethical and democratic public administration, one that recognizes its potential for evil and thereby creates greater possibilities for avoiding the many pathways toward state- sponsored dehumanization and destruction. This approach (as with any attempt to rethink aspects of the field) is bound to bring us into conflict with some of the conventional wisdom and traditions of public administration. Our critical stance toward public administration is aimed not so much at any particular formulation of the field's identity but more at what has not been written—the failure to recognize administrative evil as part and parcel of the identity of public administration. Although it has had virtually no place in the field's literature, administrative evil is as much a part of public administration as other well-worn concepts such as efficiency, effectiveness, accountability, and productivity.

Failing to See Administrative Evil

A lack of attention to what we believe to be a vitally important concept can be explained by the understandable, yet unfortunate, tendency to lament acts of administrative evil while dismissing them as temporary and isolated aberrations or deviations from proper administrative behavior. In considering eruptions of evil throughout history, it is commonplace to think of them as emanating from a unique context. We want to believe that they occur at a particular historical moment and within a specific culture. Although this is clearly true, at least in part, it also holds a cunning deception: The effect of understanding great eruptions of evil as historical aberrations is that we safely wall them off from our own time and space, and from ordinary people in ordinary times.

It is not unusual for the Holocaust (and other, lesser state-sponsored atrocities) to be viewed in such terms, for example, perceiving that, in the midst of extraordinary circumstances, Hitler led Germany out of the fold of Western culture and into a deviant, criminal culture. As Rubenstein (1975) and Bauman (1989) have argued, however, the Holocaust, rather than being a deviation from Western civilization, was one of its inherent (although not inevitable) possibilities, carried out in large part by the most advanced, technical-rational mechanisms and procedures of modern civilization. Furthermore, it was the public service and advanced administrative procedures that made the mass slaughter possible:

> The Final Solution did not clash at any stage with the rational pursuit of efficient, optimal goal implementation. On the contrary, *it arose out of a genuinely rational concern, and it was generated by bureaucracy true to its form and purpose.* The Holocaust . . . was a legitimate resident in the house of modernity; indeed, one who would not be at home in any other house. (Bauman, 1989, p. 17)

The same can be said of other examples of administrative evil in the history of American government and public service, as we discuss here. We examine in Chapter 4 the administrative evil of importing hundreds of Germans—some of them "committed" Nazis and some who engaged in activities for which other Germans were convicted of war crimes—to the United States after World War II so that they could spearhead our rocket research and development. Although sometimes recognized after the fact as immoral acts and even crimes, few have been able to perceive that such administrative evil is consistent with, and even an outcome of, the technical-rational pursuit of instrumental goals in the tradition of modern civilization and administration (both public and private).

In the 20th century, modern civilization has unfolded as a paradox of unparalleled progress, order, and civility on one hand, and mass murder and barbarity on the other. Rubenstein (1975, p. 91) argues, therefore, that the Holocaust "bears witness to the advance of civilization," where progress is Janus-like, with two faces, one benevolent, the other destructive. For a profession like public administration (and other professions in public life) to identify itself exclusively with the face that represents order, efficiency, productivity, creativity, and the great achievements of modern civilization is, in effect, to mask the existence of a fundamental and recurring aspect of its own history and identity—the destructive and even evil face.

> The world of the death camps and the society it engenders reveals the progressively intensifying night side of Judeo-Christian civilization. Civilization means slavery, wars, exploitation, and death camps. It also means medical hygiene, elevated religious ideas, beautiful art, and exquisite music. It is an error to imagine that civilization and savage cruelty are antithesis. . . . In our times, the cruelties, like most other aspects of our world, have become far more effectively administered than ever before. They have not and will not cease to exist. Both creation and destruction are inseparable aspects of what we call civilization. (Rubenstein, 1975, p. 195)

Robert Bellah (1971) reached similar conclusions about contemporary American culture in reflections prompted by the massacre of hundreds of civilians, mostly women and children, by American soldiers in the Vietnamese hamlet of My Lai. He stated that "both the assertion of the fundamental unity of man and the assertion that whole groups of people are defective and justly subject to extreme aggression are genuinely part of our tradition" (p. 178). From this perspective, there are not two American traditions, one good and another evil, but one tradition consisting of a paradox wherein progress in technology and human rights is accompanied by brutality, exploitation, and even mass murder. Just as Thomas Mann observed that the demonic and supremely creative were entwined in the German soul (Bellah, 1971), so freedom and exploitation are entwined in the heart of America. Likewise, public administration cannot, in the

light of this realization, be described only in terms of progress in the "art, science and profession" of administration
(see, for example, Lynn, 1996) without recognizing that acts
of administrative evil are something other than uncontrolled,
sporadic deviations from the norms of technical-rational administrative practice. Practitioners and scholars of public
administration, as well as of other related fields and professions, need to recognize that the pathways to administrative
evil are not built from the outside by seductive leaders but
emanate from within, ready to coax and nudge administrators down a surprisingly familiar route first toward moral
inversion, then to complicity in crimes against humanity.

Understanding Evil

We know that human beings are killers. We are (at least
most of us) meat eaters who must kill for the sustenance of
life. We are in the food chain and, if nothing else, we are at
minimum killers of plant life. We have learned, during the
course of human history, to kill as well for high social
purposes, that is, for political, religious, and/or economic
beliefs and systems. As uncomfortable to acknowledge as it
may be, evil is as close to all of us as ourselves.

Most versions of psychology, from Freud to Jung and
beyond, account for the potentially destructive tendencies
of human behavior, including aggression, anger, and rage.
Melanie Klein (1964), perhaps the preeminent object-relations
psychologist, understands aggression, and other emotions
as well, as relationships with "objects" (which are in most
cases other human beings). As Greenberg and Mitchell
(1983, p. 139) point out, "Drives, for Klein, are relationships." One such manifestation is hating those we love the
most (as infants and children). Such a psychic contradiction
is emotional dynamite and is defused through "splitting."

Unlike repression, which drives unwanted or intolerable emotions underground—into the unconscious—splitting is a device that allows these contradictory feelings to coexist, albeit separately, in the human consciousness. Normally, the good aspect is held internally and the bad aspect is split off, projected outward to some external person (the "object"). This is known as "projective identification." Developmentally, these phenomena interact in the following way:

> Primal splitting-and-idealization thus involves a delicate balancing act. Too little, and the child cannot protect itself from its own aggression, living in constant fear that its bad objects will overcome its good ones, and itself. Too much separation, on the other hand, will prevent the good and bad object from ever being recognized as one, an insight that is the foundation of the depressive position, in which the child despairs of ever being able to restore to wholeness the good object, which he now recognizes is inseparable from the bad object that he has destroyed in fantasy a thousand times. For Klein, the depressive position is not an illness, but a crucial step in emotional development, by which love and hate are integrated. (Alford, 1990, p. 11)

However true to life one wishes to consider object-relations psychology to the inner workings of the infant mind (and there is controversy over this issue), for our purposes, what is important is the way these insights help us understand the construction of social and organizational evil in adults.

Organizations, social institutions, and even countries can be holding environments (or "containers") for both good and evil purposes. After all, it was a church organization that conceived and carried out the many inquisitions in centuries past. When an organization, institution, or polity "contains" the unintegrated aggression and rage (the projective identification of the split-off "bad" parts) of its members, one has the phenomenon identified in the title of a book by Vamik

Volkan (1988), *The Need to Have Enemies and Allies.* The belief system, or ideology, that is manifested by the organization or polity gives the anxiety (which results from the unintegrated aggression) a name and mitigates it by making it less confusing whom to love and whom to hate. In essence, the organization or polity communicates some version (that varies according to the nature of the felt anxiety) of the following to its individual members:

> You really are being persecuted. Let me help you by naming your persecutors, and telling you who your true friends are, friends who are also being attacked by these persecutors. Together you and your true friends can fight the persecutors, and praise each other's righteousness, which will help you realize that the source of aggression and evil is out there, in the real world. And you thought it was all in your head. (Alford, 1990, p. 13)

The organization or polity has reduced the members' anxiety but reinforced the splitting off of the bad object(s) and the projective identification. Thus, the unintegrated hatred and aggression that is the source of evil is called out and is given organization and direction. This dynamic may be as benign as an amateur softball team, which makes its rival teams into "enemies." When combined with a moral inversion, in which the bad becomes good, this dynamic can lead to eruptions of evil (Alford, 1990): "To seek to destroy the bad object with all the hatred and aggression at one's command becomes good, because doing so protects the self from badness" (p. 15). From the perspective of object-relations psychology, unintegrated rage and aggression—part of the normal repertoire of human emotional responses—represent the source of evil. There may be other and perhaps better explanations, but this one provides a foundation from which we can build and elaborate more of the social and organizational dynamics of evil behavior.

Perspective and Distance

In recognizing when evil has been done, the perspective of the victim has authority. It is the body or psyche of the victim (and sometimes both) that has been marked by evil. The witness and testimony of the victim(s) carry moral authority as well and provide the foundation from which our judgments of good and evil can be made. Still, there is a distortion from the victim's perspective. From the victim's perspective, an act of cruelty or violence (or the perpetrator of that act—or both) typically is described as evil—most typically, as wholly evil. Baumeister (1997) refers to this as the "myth of pure evil" (p. 17).

The myth of pure evil is compounded by at least two related tendencies. First, the psychological concept of splitting, as discussed above, projects those aspects of the psyche seen as "all bad" outward onto some object (typically a person or persons). Second, American culture, for example, has a propensity, considerably exacerbated by popular media and particularly by television, to cast moral questions in black and white, all good or all bad terms. Villains are thus wholly evil, and we have no tolerance for a hero who is not all good. In the political arena, we ask that national leaders have a flawless and spotless past. The myth of pure evil thus represents a dangerous propensity to cast moral questions in absolute terms, which in turn makes them easier to reverse, leading to moral inversion.

The perpetrator's description of the same act differs from that of the victim, often dramatically. Baumeister refers to this as the *magnitude gap*:

> The importance of what takes place is almost always much greater for the victim than for the perpetrator. When trying to understand evil, one is always asking, "How could they do such a horrible thing." But the horror is usually being measured in the victim's terms. To the perpetrator, it is often

a very small thing. As we saw earlier, perpetrators generally have less emotion about their acts than do victims. It is almost impossible to submit to rape, pillage, impoverishment or possible murder without strong emotional reactions, but it is quite possible to perform those crimes without emotion. In fact, it makes it easier in many ways. (1997, p. 18)

The magnitude gap is centrally important in seeking to understand evil. From the victims' perspective and most often in hindsight, evil is more readily identified. From the perspective of the perpetrator, however, the recognition of evil is problematic. From the perpetrator's perspective, the act of cruelty or violence was perhaps "not so good" (not to say, evil), but considering other factors, such as prior injustices or some provocation, perpetrators rather easily produce rationales and justifications for even the most heinous acts (Baumeister, 1997, p. 307): "The combination of desire and minimally plausible evidence is a powerful recipe for distorted conclusions." The importance of *perspective* in recognizing evil may be captured by an old adage: Whether one sees evil depends upon where one stands. One can only "stand" elsewhere by a mental act of critical reflexivity, in which one has to reflect critically on one's own position, entailing both a recognition of context and empathy—seeing from the perspective of others.

Distance also is important, in terms of both space and time. It is clearly more difficult to name evil, and do so convincingly, in one's own historical time period. Consider the recent genocide in Rwanda and ethnic cleansing in the former Yugoslavia. Even from the distant perspective of a concerned nation—the United States—evidence during the time of those events was spotty. Although we would argue that the evidence was sufficient for the United States to have taken stronger action than it did, the point is that a social or political consensus is not so easily achieved when events are unfolding and the situation is murky. In hindsight, and when we are no longer called on to do anything, it is much easier to name such events as evil with very widespread agreement (but only if a Serb and Bosnian, or Hutu and Tutsi, are not part of the discourse). Geographic and cultural (or racial) distance matter as well. The Rwandan genocide was horrific, but after all, it was in Africa. Bosnia was murkier, more difficult, because it was in the West, in Europe. Naming the Holocaust as evil is made easier because it was the Germans who perpetrated it , but even so, it took the passage of nearly 25 years before there was much discussion of this signal event in the United States (Hilberg, 1985).

Both distance and perspective are powerful constituents of the mask of administrative evil. Naming any evil that American public administrators have done, even many years ago, is made more difficult because we have no distance from our own culture and profession. To recognize administrative evil in our own time is most problematic of all, because we have neither distance nor perspective without an explicit and somewhat difficult effort to create them (critical reflexivity). In subsequent chapters, we will name evil done by public administrators, but there will be no easy agreement, on the part of at least some readers, with our diagnosis. Unmasking administrative evil in our time and in our culture is fraught with difficulty because, in essence, we wear the mask.

Language and Dehumanization

Given that much of what we do on a daily basis is taken for granted or tacit (Polanyi, 1966), two additional elements make us especially susceptible to participation in evil, without us "knowing" what we are doing. The first of these is *language*. The use of euphemism or of technical language often helps provide emotional distance from what we are really doing (Orwell, 1950/1984). "Collateral damage" from bombing raids is a euphemism for killing civilian noncombatants and reducing nonmilitary property to rubble. In the Holocaust, code words were used for killing: "evacuation," "special treatment," and the now well-known "final solution." In cases of moral inversion, language can prevent us from connecting our actions with our normal, moral categories of right and wrong, of good and evil. The annihilation of a town—that is, the uprooting of an entire community, the expropriation of its property, and its evacuation to forced labor or death camps— was called "resettlement" or "labor in the East." Such language provided the minimal evidence needed to convince people that not only was such activity *not* evil, but it was socially appropriate or even necessary. *Language* often masks administrative evil.

Dehumanization is another powerful ally in the conduct of evil. If one does something cruel or violent to a fellow human being, it may well be morally disturbing, but if that person is part of a group of people who are (that is, have been redefined as) not "normal," not like the majority, or not good Americans, such action becomes easier. If those people can be defined as less than human, "all bad," rather like bugs or roaches (a classic moral inversion), extermination can all too easily be seen as the appropriate action. "They" brought it on themselves, after all. As Albert Speer, Hitler's minister of armaments, said about Jews (Speer, 1970), "If I had continued to see them as human beings, I would not have remained a Nazi. I did not hate them. I was indifferent to them" (p. 315). *Dehumanization* also often masks administrative evil.

The Taken for Granted

Tacit knowing—the taken for granted nature of our daily habits of action—is essential to our ability to function in a social world (Polanyi, 1966) in which even the simplest activity is enormously and dauntingly complex if each component and step had to be. articulated and thought about explicitly. The taken for granted also bears on our human capacity to participate in evil, as Baumeister notes:

> Another factor that reduces self-control and fosters the crossing of moral boundaries is a certain kind of mental state. This state is marked by a very concrete, narrow, rigid way of thinking, with the focus on the here and now, on the details of what one is doing. It is the state that characterizes someone who is fully absorbed in working with tools or playing a video game. One does not pause to reflect on broader implications or grand principles or events far removed in time (past or future). (1997, p. 268)

Most of our daily lives in social institutions and organizations is taken for granted. Not only do we not stop and think about everything that we do (which would socially paralyze us), but we hardly stop and think about anything. We do not have to make a decision about which side of the road we will drive on when we start our automobile; indeed, "side of the road" does not come up on our conscious "radar screen." In most of what we do on a daily or routine basis, we are simply engaged in well-worn habits of action. There is nothing to prompt us to stop and question. So it is with administrative evil. In a culture that emphasizes technical rationality, being "at work" for most means being narrowly focused on the task at hand. This is our typical focus of awareness, which drives out, or at least minimizes, our subsidiary awareness of ethics and morality (and other contextual matters as well). Acts of administrative evil are all too easily taken for granted as well.

The Social Construction of Evil

Individualism, one of the core values of American culture, is a barrier to our understanding of group and organizational dynamics— and administrative evil. In our culture, we are inclined to assume that each individual's actions are freely and independently chosen. When we examine an individual's behavior in isolation or even in aggregate, as we often do, that notion can be reinforced. Our culture's emphasis on individualism blinds us to group and organizational dynamics, which typically play a powerful role in shaping human behavior.

It is an easy to make—but important—error to personalize evil in the form of the exceptional psychopath, such as Charles Manson or Jeffrey Dahmer (often without considering how they might be a product of our culture). This proclivity draws a cloak over social and organizational evil. The term "mob psychology," however, still has a resonance for most. We have a long history in the United States of public lynching, clearly a recurring example of social evil. Even more to the point, thousands of people have been subjected to administrative evil in dehumanizing experiments, internment in camps, and other destructive acts by public agencies often done in the name of science and/or the national interest (Nevitt & Comstock, 1971; Stannard, 1992).

As we argue in Chapter 2, public administration and the social sciences have been dominated by the scientific-analytic mind-set. We have approached social and political problems with the tools of science, thinking of social and human phenomena as if they had the same tangibility and properties as physical reality. Societies and cultures, however, are human artifacts, created and enacted by human activities through time. Social and political institutions—

indeed, all human organizations—are thus socially constructed (Berger & Luckmann, 1967). This means, of course, that they are not immutable; what human beings create and enact can be reenacted in some different way. This does not mean, however, that organizations and institutions are easily malleable.

To say that human social and cultural institutions and organizations are socially constructed may seem to imply that at some point groups of people rationally choose to meet together, and they consciously and intentionally set about to devise an institution. Such an activity, of course, is the very rare exception. Rather, organizations and institutions more typically emerge a little bit at a time. As children, we are socialized into a culture that already has a vast array of institutions, practices, and "rules of the road." For the most part, these come to feel natural to us, or more aptly, second nature. During a person's lifetime, most organizations or institutions will change, but usually not dramatically. Still, they *could* change dramatically. Revolutions, economic depressions, and even natural cataclysms can prompt rapid and dramatic change in a society, and of course there are new institutions. Television is a social institution that has developed within the lifetime of many still alive. The Internet seems well on the way to developing into a social institution.

Another core value of American culture is the rule of law, based in part on the sanctity of contracts. The commercial application of such a core value may be of primary importance, but we should not overlook its social manifestation. Our political and legal systems provide the foundation for law and order in social terms. When the public order is perceived to be threatened, as it is in the contemporary atmosphere of fear of crime and random violence, the response of the citizenry is visceral, if arguably off target—solve the problem by building more prisons, instituting longer prison terms, and bringing back the death penalty while speeding up the execution process. The powerful social motivation for the preservation of social order is fueled by a fear of chaotic conditions. This fundamental need for social order helps in understanding just how strong the inclination to obey authority is for most people. Compliance accounts of human behavior thus help us understand how ordinary social life is maintained over time (stopping at traffic lights magnified into thousands of daily social interactions). Two experiments in the social construction of compliance help us see both what we may typically overlook and how it is that ordinary people can be caught up in administrative evil.

The Social Construction of Compliance

In the mid-1960s, Professor Stanley Milgram of Yale University placed an advertisement in the New Haven, Connecticut, newspaper seeking volunteers for a "study of memory" (Milgram, 1974). Volunteers were promised payment of $4 for their time and trouble. As the experiment began in the Psychology Department at Yale, each participant found himself (the initial experiments' subjects were all males) in a room with a "scientist in a white coat," who ran the experiment, and another participant, who actually was an actor. The "scientist" explained that the experiment was a study of memory in which there would be a "teacher" and a "learner." The other "subject," the actor, was chosen through a rigged lottery to be the "learner," always leaving the only real participant in the role of "teacher."

The role of the "teacher" was to read a series of word pairs to the "learner," who then attempted to recite them from memory. A correct answer was simply acknowledged, but upon hearing an incorrect answer, the "teacher's" task was to press the button on the rather elaborate console in front of him, which delivered an electric shock to the "learner."

The "teacher" was given a 45 volt shock before beginning the questions, so as to have some direct sense of the learner's experience. A 45 volt shock is sufficient to get one's attention. That was the only real electric shock anyone actually received in the experiment, but the "teacher" did not know this and acted under the assumption that he was actually administering a series of shocks to the "learner." The "learner" was literally strapped into a chair, with electrodes attached to one bare arm.

The console of the shock generator had 30 ascending levels of shocks, starting at 15 volts and continuing in 15 volt increments all the way to 450 volts. The console was further labeled by groups, with the first group called "slight shock," the next "moderate shock," then "strong shock," which ended at 180 volts. The scale continued with "very strong shock," "intense shock," "extreme intensity shock," "danger: severe shock," and finally, the simple "XXX." It was anticipated that many subjects would express hesitations or objections as the experiment progressed and they were called upon to deliver ever-increasing shocks. A series of "prods" was established, such that the first time the "teacher" expressed hesitation, the "scientist in the white coat" said "Please continue." After the next three such expressions by the "teacher," the remaining three prods in order were "The experiment requires that you continue," "It is absolutely essential that you continue," and "You have no other choice, you must go on." A fifth balk by the "teacher" terminated the experiment.

Professor Milgram had the thought of asking several different samples of people what they thought the subjects' response in this experimental situation would be. He asked samples of psychiatrists, graduate students, sophomores, and a middle-class group from New Haven what they thought. To a person, they indicated that they personally would break off at some point early in the experiment, and they predicted that only a pathological few subjects in a thousand would deliver shocks all the way to 450 volts.

Although the experiment came to have many variants, the initial one was the so-called voice-proximity version. In this version, the "learner" was positioned in a room adjacent to the "teacher," but with the door open, so his voice could be heard. The "learner" of course rapidly began giving far more incorrect responses on the word-pair questions, and at the fifth level (75 volts), he grunted audibly. At 120 volts, the "learner" complained verbally that the shocks were painful. Two levels later, at 150 volts, the "learner" demanded release. At 270 volts, the "learner" began delivering an agonized scream after each shock, and from 300 to 330 volts, no answer was offered, only the scream. The "scientist in the white coat" explained that no answer was to be considered as an incorrect answer. After 330 volts, there was no further response from the learner at all.

In the voice-proximity version, fully 62.5% of the subjects went through all 30 levels on the console, delivering the final two shocks of 435 and 450 volts in the XXX category. If one used the willingness to deliver a "strong shock" of 135 volts as the measure of compliance, then fully 99% of the subjects complied. Remember, at 120 volts, the "learner" complained about the pain of the shocks. In other versions of the experiment—for example, moving the "learner" into the same room as the "teacher"—the percentage of fully obedient subjects was reduced but was still at 40%. No version of this experiment of which we are aware—Milgram's or others'—has produced what we would call comforting results.

This kind of experiment would never pass muster before a human subjects review panel today. The "scientist" and the "learner" misrepresent themselves, the entire situation is a fabrication, and in general the subject is lied to by the person in authority. Still, the "teacher" finds himself in a rather typical social situation. A legitimate authority figure, a "scientist," backed by the stature of a major university, presents an experiment that ostensibly will help to discover more about learning. The learner is a volunteer, just like the teacher. When the situation induced discomfort, which it did for large numbers of participants, the "scientist" authoritatively took full responsibility for the experiment and its consequences. Once the procedure began—15 volts is insignificant—role acceptance was in place, and the situation was loaded so that a clear and strong individual response was needed to break free of the setting. In this culture, which so highly values individualism, our expectation is that the individual response will trump the social situation and nearly everyone will break off—and most assuredly not fully comply. We find instead that these Americans were perfectly willing to play the role of "shock technician" or perhaps even "executioner," as long as the role was euphemistically called "teacher" and someone in a position of authority took full responsibility. In at least this context, and perhaps in others, American culture seems well adapted for administrative evil.

The Stanford Prison Experiment

A second experiment in compliance, this one conducted in the basement of the Psychology Department at Stanford University, produced equally disturbing results (Haney, Banks, & Zimbardo, 1974). The three psychology professors selected 22 of the most normal male undergraduates they could find at Stanford. They specifically tested for individual "dispositional characteristics" that might have inclined subjects toward higher degrees of either passive or aggressive behavior. The plan was to create a simulated prison in the basement of their building in which 11 subjects were randomly assigned to be prisoners, and 11 others to be guards (with two in each group to be backups in case of illness).

Nine prisoners were to occupy three cells in groups of three, and the nine guards were divided equally into three 8-hour shifts.

The "contract" offered to the subjects at the beginning of the experiment gave assurances of adequate diet, clothing, housing, and medical care—and more generally, "humane conditions." Prisoners were told they could expect to be under surveillance and have some basic civil rights suspended, but that there would be no physical abuse. Direction for the guards was simple: "Maintain the reasonable degree of order within the prison necessary for its effective functioning." Prisoners were provided a loose, muslin smock with a number on the front and back, no underclothes, a light chain and lock around one ankle, rubber sandals, and a nylon stocking skull cap. Guards were given a uniform of plain khaki shirts and pants, a whistle, a police nightstick, and reflecting sunglasses (making eye contact impossible). The Palo Alto police department helped out by "arresting" each prisoner and running them through all the standard booking procedures. The situation was loaded with social cues to mimic the experience of prison, but unlike the Milgram experiments, here there was no "scientist" or other authority figure who stood ready to assume the responsibility for the choices made by the participants.

Prisoners followed rules that were developed by the guards: three supervised toilet visits per day, 2 hours for reading or letter writing, work assignments (to "earn" the $15 per day that all participants were paid), two visiting periods per week, movie rights, and exercise periods. Three times a day, at the beginning of each shift, there was a lineup for a "count" (with nine prisoners, this was hardly difficult). The first of these lasted 10 minutes, but these were spontaneously increased in length by the guards, until some lasted several hours. Interactions between guards and prisoners quickly assumed a negative tone, with prisoners assuming a passive, sullen role and guards an aggressive, initiating role that became characterized by verbal affronts.

Total guard aggression increased daily, even after prisoners had ceased any resistance, and deterioration was visible. Prisoner rights were redefined as privileges, to be earned by obedient behavior. The experiment was planned for 2 weeks but was terminated after 6 days. Five prisoners were released because of extreme emotional depression, crying, rage, and/or acute anxiety. Guards forced the prisoners to chant filthy songs, to defecate in buckets that were not emptied, and to clean toilets with their bare hands. They acted as if the prisoners were less than human, and so did the prisoners:

> At the end of only six days we had to close down our mock prison because what we saw was frightening. It was no longer apparent to us or most of the subjects where they ended and their roles began. The majority had indeed become "prisoners" or "guards," no longer able to clearly differentiate between role-playing and self. There were dramatic changes in virtually every aspect of their behavior, thinking and feeling. In less than a week, the experience of imprisonment undid (temporarily) a lifetime of learning; human values were suspended, self-concepts were challenged, and the ugliest, most base, pathological side of human nature surfaced. We were horrified because we saw some boys ("guards") treat other boys as if they were despicable animals, taking pleasure in cruelty, while other boys ("prisoners") became servile, dehumanized robots who thought only of escape, of their own individual survival, and of their mounting hatred of the guards. (Haney et al., 1974, p. 94)

Taken together, these two experiments suggest that social roles and social structures play a far more powerful part in everyday human behavior than our American belief in individualism can admit. We can see clearly how individual morality can be swallowed and effectively erased by social roles and structures (Kelman & Hamilton, 1989). Technical rationality, professionalism, and bureaucracy all redefine ethics out of the picture in many instances. One is rarely confronted with a clear, "up or down" decision on an ethical issue; rather, a series of small, usually ambiguous choices are made, and the weight of commitments and of habit drives out morality. The skids are further greased if the situation is defined or presented as technical, or calling for expert judgment, or is legitimated by organizational authority. It becomes an even easier choice if the immoral choice has itself been redefined, through a moral inversion, as the "good" or "right" thing to do.

Individual, Organization, and Society

So far, we have seen how our cultural predispositions can blind us to aspects of human behavior that are crucial in understanding administrative evil. How do we develop these behavioral tendencies and bring them to organizations, and how do these dynamics link with our larger social and cultural context? These connections are the topic of Shapiro and Carr's book, *Lost in Familiar Places: Creating New Connections Between the Individual and Society* (1991). Both families and organizations, along with other social institutions, are *familiar* places for us; after all, we spend our lives in them. As the authors note, however, we increasingly experience a sense of strangeness in these places; hence, the "lost in familiar places" refrain. Old ways of understanding what a family is, for example, seem overwhelmed by changes that affect the ways in which, over time, we negotiate a sense of meaning in our lives. The old anchors do not reach bottom, and we are cast adrift. A more or less stable, shared understanding of the family or of the church or of the work organization in the past served in part as a buffer for the ideology of individualism so pervasive in American society. For most of us, our socialization into various institutions is no longer "automatic," and the socialization that we do receive is increasingly fragmented and complex.

Shapiro and Carr discuss meaning, and in particular the process by which we develop meaning, as negotiated collaborative interpretation—a fundamentally relational process. They focus on the primary human group—the family— as the context in which we first learn this process, and as providing the initial model with which we subsequently attempt to make meaningful sense out of organizational life. As they develop a phenomenology of family life, the authors suggest that curiosity is a central constant in healthy families; that is, the parents' (or caregivers') stance toward the child is captured by the question "What is your experience?" rather than by versions of the command "Your experience is. . . ." The question builds, over time, a capacity for negotiated, collaborative interpretation (the child pieces together boundaries that define "who I am"), whereas the command cuts off negotiation and imposes a definition of self on the child, leading potentially to a fragmented, defensive, and often neurotic personality. In this case, the child is apt to carry unintegrated rage and aggression into adult life, along with its characteristic splitting and projective identification.

Alternatively, the split good and bad objects can be successfully reintegrated into the self, which may lead to reparation. Reparation is the motivation in mature human beings to complete worthy tasks and to make things whole again, and to do so in the recognition that there is capacity for both great good and great evil in each of us. This, then, is a recognition that moves one past splitting and projective identification, processes we learn as children as a means of coping with the otherwise unbearable knowledge that we experience hate and rage toward those we love, and the concomitant anxiety that those feelings induce. Alternatively, destructive patterns of interaction quite common in organizational life enable us to maintain the projections we grew used to as children, or even to be ready accomplices to administrative evil.

Shapiro and Carr go on to make interesting linkages to broader social institutions, such as religion. Here the key concept is the notion of a "holding environment" (or "container"), which has to do with how families (or other organizations) manage the emotional issues of their members. In the successful holding environment, empathic interpretation, valuing the experiences of others, and containment of aggression and sexuality are managed in ways that sustain the integrity of members. Organizations, social institutions, and countries also function as holding environments or containers. Religious institutions may be thought of as ritualized symbolic structures that contain chaotic experiences; that is, they act as holding environments for these difficult feelings and emotions (Shapiro & Carr, 1991). "Our proposition is that a key holding environment is continually being negotiated and created through the unconscious interaction between members of a society and its religious institutions" (p. 159). As we have seen, however, organizations, institutions, and countries also serve as holding environments for evil. People who need direction—a target, really—for their unintegrated rage and aggression, who must split off the "bad" and project it outward, hear all too well the siren call of groups and organizations that will contain this psychic energy for them. The price tag is almost always obedience and loyalty, and sometimes moral inversion; occasionally, the price tag is very dear indeed—those truly evil eruptions that become the great moral debacles of human history.

2

The Framework of Administrative Evil

Modernity and Technical Rationality

No one knows who will live in this cage in the future, or whether at the end of this tremendous development entirely new prophets will arise, or there will be a great rebirth of old ideas and ideals, or, if neither, mechanized petrification, embellished with a sort of convulsive self-importance. For of the last stage of this cultural development, it might well be truly said: "Specialists without spirit, sensualists without heart; this nullity imagines that is has attained a level of civilization never before achieved."

—*Max Weber (1905/1958, p. 182)*

◆ This chapter seeks to provide an analytical framework for understanding administrative evil by examining the historical context of American public administration. The most important aspect of the historical context is the culture at large within which public administration is practiced, researched, and taught. Today, the culture at large may be characterized as one of *modernity* (Turner, 1990; see also

Bauman, 1989; Bernstein, 1985; Rabinbach, 1990). Modernity is the culmination of a centuries-long process of modernization. Intellectual strands of modernity reach back to the 16th and 17th centuries, but as the defining characteristic of our own culture, modernity coalesced only within the past century. Modernity describes a social, political, and economic world increasingly characterized by "secularization, the universalistic claims of instrumental rationality, the differentiation of the various spheres of the life-world, the bureaucratization of economic, political and military practices, and the growing monetarization of values" (Turner, 1990, p. 6).

Our culture of modernity has as one of its chief constituents *technical rationality* (Barrett, 1979). Technical rationality is a way of thinking and living that emphasizes the scientific-analytical mind-set and the belief in technological progress. In the United States, the cornerstone of technical rationality was laid down just before and during the Progressive Era (1896-1920). A confluence of two streams occurred during this period that unleashed a whole set of ideas and practices into the social and political world (Wiebe, 1967, pp. 145-163). One of the two streams emerged from the recent history of epistemology in Western culture. This first stream is the scientific-analytical mind-set that was the legacy of 17th-century Enlightenment thinking. The second stream was the product of the Great Transformation of the 19th century and comprised the technological progress characteristic of this period of industrialization, with its unparalleled succession of technological developments. We elaborate further on the emergence and development of technical rationality below, but first an overview of the argument is provided.

The argument in this chapter proceeds as follows. We examine first the state of historical scholarship within the field of public administration. Concentrating on modernity leads to a primary focus on the period just before and during the Progressive Era, when, it is argued, the essential parameters of modern public administration emerged. The development of technical rationality, along with professionalism and the emphasis on science and efficiency, is closely examined. Next, we suggest that the belief system of technical rationality accounts for the lack of a historical consciousness in social science in general and public administration in particular. We then discuss the implications of the lack of a historical consciousness for public administration theory and practice. In spite of considerable historical research, the field of public administration continues to echo themes of technical rationality in repeated calls for professionalism and for more "rigorous" and "scientific" research. These calls for professionalism and research reflect, in part, a blindness to the existence and importance of administrative evil. We link these questions pertaining to public administration to the culture at large, encompassing both a political dimension and an epistemological dimension. Given the historical context of modernity—a context of technical rationality—the prospects for the future of administrative evil and public administration are discussed. We begin with an overview of historical studies in the field.

Historical Studies in Public Administration

Attention to the historical roots of public administration has ebbed and flowed in the last half century. Dwight Waldo's *The Administrative State* (1948) is still clearly the seminal work on the larger cultural context of American public administration. Well into the post-World War II era, those looking to public administration history found little beyond Leonard D. White's four volumes (1948, 1951, 1954, 1958) on the development of public administration institutions, although Paul P. Van Riper's *A History of the U.S. Civil Service* (1958) appeared in the same year as White's last volume. The decade of the 1960s saw the publication of Frederick C. Mosher's *Democracy and the Public Service* (1968), along with two historical studies of the civil service (Aronson, 1964; Hoogenboom, 1961). The benchmarks of the 1970s were David H. Rosenbloom's *Federal Service and the Constitution* (1971) and a pair of articles, one by Lynton K. Caldwell (1976) and the other by Barry D. Karl (1976), in the bicentennial issue of *Public Administration Review*. An important book by Stephen Skowronek, *Building a New American State* (1982), appeared early in the next decade but received spotty attention in the public administration literature. Later in the same decade, Ralph Clark Chandler's *A Centennial History of the American Administrative State* (1987) represented a significant contribution.

Some research on the historical development of public administration has focused on the Founding Period, which is one of the key periods for the understanding of contemporary public administration. John A. Rohr's work (1986; see also 1985) on the constitutional basis for public administration is a prominent example. More recently, this period was the focus of O. C. McSwite's (1997) *Legitimacy in Public Administration*. Some have appropriately focused attention on the writing of Alexander Hamilton, who stands out among the Founders for his attention to matters related to public administration, and certainly for his relevance to the later development of public administration (Green, 1990; see also Caldwell, 1990).

The tension between democracy and administration, both as they were construed in the American founding and as their meaning has altered through time, has powerfully affected how the public sector in the United States has evolved. An article by Laurence J. O'Toole, Jr. (1987), illustrates how this tension manifested in the doctrines of separation of powers beginning with the Founding Period, and later in the Progressive Era in the politics-administration dichotomy. The linkage between the Founding Period and the Progressive Era has also been emphasized in a piece by Jeffrey L. Sedgwick (1987; see also 1986) that focuses on similarities in the theories of administration between the Founders and Woodrow Wilson. Both of these articles show clearly the relevance of these historical periods for contemporary thought in public administration. The focus here on modernity suggests further discussion of the period just before and during the Progressive Era, to which we now turn.

The Progressive Era:
A Second Hamiltonian System

The dominant image of the Progressive Era, the period from 1896 to 1920, is perhaps still the age of reform (Hofstadter, 1955). The Progressive Era was a time of popular outrage against the depredations of big business, against social ills, and against exploitation of all kinds. The result was a wave of progressive reform—child labor legislation, the minimum wage, women's suffrage, direct election of senators, the income tax, trust busting—as well as eliminating patronage, instituting clean government, and regulating industry. The image obscures as much as it reveals.

The Progressive Era saw Jeffersonian language emphasizing a laissez-faire, limited government used by conservative businessmen (especially small businessmen; Weinstein, 1968). The reformers, on the other hand, used Hamiltonian language, promoting an active, assertive national government in the service of not just economic aims but social principles as well. The Progressive aim was a Hamiltonian national government in the service of Jeffersonian ideals. In many instances, this was altered in practice to become a Hamiltonian national government with Jeffersonian rhetoric in the service of commercial interests. Gabriel Kolko (1963) aptly called this age of "reform," the "triumph of conservatism." Clientele agencies such as the Department of Commerce, which was formed in 1913, straightforwardly served their "client's" interests. Regulatory agencies, created in response to public outcry, often became, to all intents and purposes, client agencies of the regulated (Nelson, 1982).

The Progressive Era
Legacy for Public Administration

There has been considerable attention paid in the public administration literature to the Progressive Era. This period of time is widely acknowledged as the beginning of public administration as a field of study, with Woodrow Wilson, a prominent Progressive himself, almost universally cited as the founder of modern public administration (Walker, 1990; see also Link, 1964). The 20-year period before the Progressive Era (1877-1896), during which the civil service reformers were active, must also be included as central to the development of modern public administration (Rosenbloom, 1971). The civil service reformers set the stage for important developments that came together later in the Progressive Era. Two of the strongest historical analyses (Skowronek, 1982; Wiebe, 1967) use 1877 as the beginning date and 1920 as the end date. There is no inclination here to conflate long-term historical trends definitively within the 20-year bounds of the Progressive Era. The end of Reconstruction in 1877 and the close of World War I in 1920 represent about as clearly defined boundaries as one can achieve with historical analysis.

With some noteworthy exceptions, however, most contemporary public administration literature leaps immediately from Wilson's time to the New Deal era of the 1930s, or to the World War II period, when, it is thought, institutions and practices that most closely resemble the present ones came together (Henry, 1990). Most often in the public administration literature, a ritual mention of Wilson is followed by a jump to the present time, with no historical analysis at all.

The legacy of the period before and during the Progressive Era for contemporary thought in public administration is considerably greater than generally acknowledged. As Laurence J. O'Toole, Jr. (1984), persuasively argues, basic reform principles and practices endemic in the public administration literature date from the Progressive days. The "new public administration," he argues, rather than springing *de novo* from the ethos of the 1960s, shares the same ideology of reform that was elaborated at the turn of the century. We want to argue here that the fundamental trajectory of public administration theory and practice dates from the period 1877-1920 as well. First, the importance of the period before and during the Progressive Era for contemporary public administration needs some elaboration.

The broad structural and ideological outlines of the modern welfare liberal state came together in the Progressive Era, rather than much later as the conventional wisdom has it. As Weinstein puts it (1968, p. ix), "the political ideology now dominant in the United States, and the broad programmatic outlines of the liberal state (known by such names as the New Freedom, the New Deal, the New Frontier and the Great Society) were worked out and, in part, tried out by the end of the First World War." A similar argument, made in part by Skowronek (1982; see also Lustig, 1982) in his *Building a New American State*, holds for public administration. The basic parameters and trajectory of the field became visible during the period just before and during the Progressive Era, and the evolution of public administration since that time, both in practice and in thought, has not deviated significantly from that framework.

Skowronek analyzes the reconstitution of the federal government during this period, reaching back to the end of Reconstruction in 1877 for the beginnings of this process (see also Higgs, 1987). This transformation began as patchwork efforts to repair first one area and then another, often in response to the political pressure brought to bear by one or another socially powerful group. These efforts often went awry (Nelson, 1982). After the watershed presidential election of 1896 between Bryan and McKinley, however, a more systematic reconstruction was undertaken. Thus, the federal government, according to Skowronek, was reconstructed during the Progressive Era to serve new goals and interests that were growing more and more important. The themes of this reconstruction were (a) the promise of a new democracy, (b) the embrace of corporate conservatism, (c) the lure of professionalism, and (d) the quest for administrative rationality (Skowronek, 1982, p. 18).

Technical Rationality and Professionalism

The scientific-analytic mind-set and technological progress that combined during the Progressive Era unleashed a powerful current of technical rationality and professionalism. Impressed by the tremendous achievements of science and technology in the physical world, the Progressives naturally wanted to apply them in the social and political world, to achieve science-like precision and objectivity in these spheres as well (Bendix, 1956; Graebner, 1987).

Technical rationality led inevitably to specialized, expert knowledge, the very lifeblood of the professional, and then to the proliferation of professional associations in the latter half of the 19th and early part of the 20th century (Larson, 1977). Without the legitimacy derived from specialized knowledge, professionals could not have gained either the social status or the autonomy and control over the practice of the profession that are the ultimate goals, even if sometimes unstated, of every profession. The compartmentalization of knowledge demanded by technical rationality also inevitably led to a contextless, or timeless, practice: Witness the lack of historical consciousness across the professions and disciplines. The practice of a profession with little or no sense of context has precluded meaningful engagement with the larger ethical and political concerns of a society (Guerreiro-Ramos, 1981). That is to say, professionalism, fed and nurtured by technical rationality, led inexorably to a naked public square. This is the antipolitical dimension of modernity (Arendt, 1954).

It is important to note here that the Progressives and the civil service reformers who preceded them were not uniform in their thought (Noble, 1958, 1970; White, 1957). There were many differences in their thinking and many strands interwoven in their debates. James Stever's work (1986, 1990), for example, points to the tension between organic idealism and scientific pragmatism, visible both in Woodrow Wilson's writing (1887) and in Mary Parker Follett's work (1918), among others. Technical rationality, with its emphasis on the application of scientific method and procedure, won the day (Miller & O'Leary, 1989).

The modern model of professionalism was conceived and tried out in the period just before and during the Progressive Era. The development of professional associations of all kinds began in the mid-19th century, at first more rapidly in England and then burgeoning in the United States (Larson, 1977, p. 246). The characteristics of professions, which are fully visible around the turn of the century, include a professional association, a cognitive scientific base, institutionalized training (usually within higher education), licensing, work autonomy, colleague control, and a code of ethics (Larson, 1977, p. 208). Larson emphasizes the connection between the development of professionalism and the broader process of modernization, "the advance of science and cognitive rationality and the progressive differentiation and rationalization of the division of labor in industrial societies" (1977, p. xiii).

Modernity and Technical Rationality

In the context of modernity, technical rationality is the convergence of the scientific-analytical mind-set and technological progress (Turner, 1990). Beginning in the Progressive Era, it was applied to the social world and placed on the political agenda. Technical rationality is quite similar to "functional rationality" as it was described by Karl Mannheim (1940). Mannheim saw functional rationality as the logical organization of tasks into smaller units, originally in the interest of efficiency. Mannheim contrasted this with "substantive rationality," the ability to understand the purposeful nature of the whole system of which a particular task is a part. Technical rationality is also closely akin to the notion of "instrumental reason" as it was discussed by Max Horkheimer (1947). Instrumental reason is the narrow application of human reason solely in the service of instrumental aims. Until the modern era, reason was conceived as a process incorporating ethical and normative concerns as well as the consideration of merely instrumental aims. In the public administration literature, similar points have been made by Alberto Guerreiro-Ramos (1981).

Recent History of Epistemology

To understand how technical rationality became pervasive in the social and political world, and therefore in the public administration world as well, a brief look at the recent history of epistemology may help. By the time of the 17th-century Enlightenment, science, as physical science, had emerged on the scene and had begun to exert a powerful influence. Epistemology became preoccupied with a quest for the irreducible facts of existence. By the 18th century, the split between European and Anglo-American epistemology and philosophy had begun to be visible (this split has blurred considerably more recently). European philosophy may be represented as a series of attempts to resuscitate epistemology and metaphysics from the problems posed by science and its method of empiricism (Hegel, 1807/1965; Heidegger, 1926/1977; Nietzsche, 1872/1956). Anglo-American philosophy, on the other hand, may be represented as a series of attempts to reconstruct the concerns of philosophy according to the insights of science and its method (Whitehead & Russell, 1910; Wittgenstein, 1922). In our culture, the scientific-analytical mind-set captured the way we think, and the study of epistemology was largely reduced to commentaries on the history of science. The scientific-analytical mind-set, then, represents one part of the confluence that occurred in the Progressive Era; technological developments comprised the other.

The Confluence of Science and Technology

The astonishing succession of technological developments during the Great Transformation of the 19th century provided the physical, tangible embodiment of the sheer power of scientific thinking. What could have been more convincing? What could have been more plausible than to apply technical rationality to the social world to achieve science-like precision and objectivity? Frederick Taylor found a ready audience for the notion of scientific management during the Progressive Era (Haber, 1964; Merkle, 1980; Noble, 1977). Technical rationality became the vehicle of hope in the social and political world, and it created a wave that before World War II prompted new professionals, managers, behaviorists, social scientists, and industrial psychologists toward a worldview in which human conflicts appeared as problems fit for engineering solutions (Bendix, 1956; see also Ellul, 1954). In our time, as William Barrett stated:

> It would be silly for anyone to announce that he is "against" technology, whatever that might mean. We should have to be against ourselves in our present historical existence. We have now become dependent upon the increasingly complex and interlocking network of production for our barest necessities. (1979, p. 229)

Building a World With No History

The tendency to ignore and downplay history and context is not unique to public administration. This impoverished historical consciousness is found across the professions and academic disciplines, and more broadly is deeply embedded in the culture at large (Smith, 1990). That part of the belief system of modernity that finds expression in technical rationality is fundamentally atemporal. Borrowing its approach from turn of the century physical science, social science remains dominantly committed to the notion of developing knowledge or certainty through atemporal causality (or the closest available approximation thereto; Faulconer and Williams, 1985). Human action is to be explained through the development of general laws and models independent of time and space. There is, in this view, no need to include history and culture in accounts of human behavior.

This somewhat bald statement of method is only rarely the overt, stated methodological or epistemological perspective of current researchers in the social sciences and in public administration. It remains deeply embedded, however, in the culture at large, in which we all participate. Although there may be impediments and some accommodations may be needed, the application of scientific method should yield up certain knowledge (or at least knowledge as certain as possible). This belief represents a root assumption of modernity within American culture and helps account for public administration's persistent atemporality, which logically entails a diminished place for historical analysis, an approach concerned fundamentally with time.

Diminished Historical Consciousness
in Public Administration

We do not wish to suggest that the scientific method was adopted within public administration (and other fields) at the turn of the century and that little has changed since then. There have been large differences within the practice of research as to what "science" and "scientific method" have meant. What has remained constant is the scientific-analytic mind-set, the attachment to application of scientific method, however defined, as the best way to knowledge by *most* researchers in the field. At the turn of the century, doing science meant in part the application of the new method of statistics. Richard Ely (1982, p. 282) in his founding statement in 1886 for the American Economic Association, called for the application of statistics, and William Allen's *Efficient Democracy* (1907) exalted the role of statistics further:

> At first glance there is hope in the far-reaching remedies suggested: universal education, referendum, manual training, proper home surroundings, opportunity for child play, wholesome recreation, civil service reform, woman suffrage, municipal ownership, Christian spirit, prohibition of the liquor traffic, doing good, electing good men to office,

etc. But important as each remedy may be, we have abun-
dant testimony that none is adequate of itself. . . . There is
one key—statistical method—which offers to trusteeship
. . . a prompt record of work accomplished and of needs
disclosed. (pp. 11-13)

The emphasis on statistics was no accident. In the classical
formulations of the 17th-century Enlightenment, science
meant a grand explanation of some aspect of nature. By the
Progressive Era, science came to mean the application of
scientific method (Wiebe, 1967, p. 147): "Science had become a procedure, or an orientation, rather than a body of
results." For many progressives, this view toward science
had its parallel with politics, which also came to be viewed
increasingly as procedural. Woodrow Wilson and Charles
Merriam are but two examples of progressives who saw a
harmonious link between the proceduralism of science and
that of politics (on Wilson, see Rabin and Bowman, 1984,
and Van Riper, 1990; for Merriam, see Karl, 1974).

Politics, especially in its democratic versions, also had to
undergo considerable revision to be made compatible with
this new emphasis on science and procedure. Herbert Croly's
writing (1909) is particularly revealing of this resolution.
The new requirements for professionalism, the demands for
expertise, the growing calls for a politics/administration
dichotomy, and the adage that there is "no Republican way
to build a road" all rendered the greater democratic involvement of people in politics more and more problematic
(Hanson, 1985). This tension between a meaningful democratic politics, on one hand, and a professionalized, scien-
tized, expert administration, on the other, has commanded
attention in the public administration literature since the
turn of the century. It was central to Waldo's *The Administrative State* (1948) and, indeed, to most of his later writing.
It has been noted more recently by Barry D. Karl (1987),
among others (see Caiden, 1984; O'Toole, 1987; Redford,

1969; Stivers, 1995), and has a central place in the recurring and persistent discussion of public administration theory and practice (Adams, Bowerman, Dolbeare, & Stivers, 1990).

Three Examples of Modernity
in Public Administration

One of the central tenets of modernity, along with technical rationality, is the notion of progress, which suggests the first example. One influential version of public administration history views the development of the field as occurring through five successive stages (Henry, 1990). The period of primary focus in Henry's chapter, the Progressive Era, is labeled the politics/ administration dichotomy. This focus was then superseded by the "principles of administration" in the 1930s, followed by public administration as political science and public administration as management in the 1950s, with the process of change culminating since 1970 in "public administration as public administration." This progression is characterized by the increasing professionalism of public administration and by its increasing development of the characteristics of an academic discipline with a scientific base. In this version, public administration has a history, but its origins, less than 100 years ago, are outmoded and have been superseded.

The 1960s, which offer the second example, saw the development of an apparently significant force in the field, the so-called new public administration (Frederickson, 1980; Marini, 1971). Ironically, the new public administration writers, many of whom explicitly saw themselves as constructing an alternative to technical rationality, were at the same time following in line with one of modernity's other central tenets, the progressive development of knowledge (O'Toole, 1984). New public administration was seen as a clear break with the orthodoxy of mainstream public administration. As O'Toole so usefully points out, however, this "break with orthodoxy" was entirely compatible with the tenets of reformism as developed in the Progressive Era. According to O'Toole, the development of public administration may best be viewed "not as successive efforts of apolitical experts to superimpose an artificial rationality on a pluralistic world, but as a continual, tension-filled struggle on the part of those who are deeply committed to some vision of democracy but who see the seeming inevitability of large-scale government bureaucracy" (1984, p. 149). Even the new public administration, which saw itself as departing from technical rationality in its "antipositivist" stance, ironically remained well within the confines of modernity. Perhaps more tellingly, the new public administration seems almost quaint from the perspective of three decades later, given the occurrence of recurring calls for greater professionalism and for greater rigor in the application of scientific method in the field (McCurdy & Cleary, 1984; Perry & Kraemer, 1986).

A third example comes from the characterization of public administration offered in Orion F. White, Jr., and Cynthia J. McSwain's (1990) "The Phoenix Project: Raising a New Image of Public Administration from the Ashes of the Past." They characterize contemporary society, as well as public administration, as dominated by what they call the "technicist episteme," roughly what we call here technical rationality. They see the technicist episteme as characteristic of modern public administration, which they date as beginning after World War II, and they contrast modern public administration with "traditional" public administration, which occurred during the 1930s and 1940s. Although their analysis of contemporary public administration and its predicament is insightful and important, their historical analysis, we would argue, is flawed. They provide a better historical analysis in a later work, which closely parallels our own (McSwite, 1997).

The central tenets they ascribe to the technicist episteme did not emerge and develop after World War II; rather, they emerged as the dominant (but not the monolithic) ideology from the Progressive experience at the turn of the century. This is not to deny the important differences from technical rationality (or in White and McSwain's terminology, the technicist episteme) exhibited by the "traditionalists." Much like the later new public administrationists, the traditionalists in part attempted to think their way out of technical rationality. Most important among these differences expressed by the traditionalists were beliefs emphasizing the political and social context and connectedness of public administration.

White and McSwain do not call for a return to "traditionalism" in public administration; rather, they investigate how traditionalist ideas can be reconstructed in ways relevant to present conditions. This proposed reconstruction is anything but sentimental, relegating a reconstituted public administration to agency "enclaves." They see very clearly the predominance of technical rationality and the difficulties of thinking and acting our way out of its confines.

It is an ironic symptom of modernity that careful analyses such as White and McSwain's do not locate accurately the crucial historical moment when modernity coalesced, and thus misconstrue the ways in which we are enthralled with modernity. Ironically, even when we construe our efforts as a departure from modernity, like the new public administrationists, we find ourselves still enmeshed in its framework. Most of the public administration literature, however, contains both less irony and less historical analysis. Modernity also has important implications for the persistent legitimacy question so often addressed in the field of public administration, to which we now turn.

Modernity, Legitimacy,
and Public Administration

Although it is clear that sufficient literature exists within the field of public administration to justify at least one chapter on the historical development of public administration, only a handful of the scores of public administration textbooks published since World War II have done so (e.g., Rosenbloom, 1989; Stillman, 1987). Virtually all such textbooks conclude, however, with a chapter on future prospects of the field, echoing modernity's theme of progress.

When public administration's historical development is mentioned, in virtually every case, Woodrow Wilson's essay (1887), "The Study of Administration," is cited. Interestingly, Van Riper (1983) recently has called its salience into serious question. He notes that Wilson's essay was not cited in the central publications of political science or public administration between 1890 and World War I, and that the article had little apparent influence until the 1950s.

Probably the next most cited historical figure in the development of public administration thought is German sociologist Max Weber (Cuff, 1978; see also Weber, 1979). His work also had minimal impact in the field until the 1950s, remaining untranslated into English until the late 1940s. Moreover, the reading of Weber's work has been selective and often out of context. In the public administration literature, the focus has been on what Weber wrote about bureaucratic organization, especially that part of it concerned with the internal organization of bureaucracies. Weber, of course, was far less concerned with the process of rationalization as it affected the internal workings of organizations than he was with the *social* implications of the process of rationalization. The former is both more consistent with modernity and far easier to treat ahistorically than the latter.

One of Weber's central themes was legitimacy, particularly legitimate authority. Clearly, as modernity was coalescing, Weber saw the increasing legitimacy of bureaucratic authority, based as it was on scientific procedure and professionalism. The issue of legitimacy has been an important one for public administration as well.

Recent discussions of legitimacy in public administration are not symptomatic of an ostensible transition to a postmodern era (Marshall & White, 1990); rather, they are simply the latest versions of attempts to reconcile the tensions between democracy and administration endemic to a liberal state (Stillman, 1991). These tensions date from the American founding, but they are brought to the forefront and exacerbated by modernity and become more prominent during and after the Progressive Era. Waldo's *The Administrative State* (1948) is a thorough analysis of these tensions covering the first half of the 20th century. Later versions raise and extend the same themes (Karl, 1987; Kass & Catron, 1990; O'Toole, 1987; Wamsley, 1990).

Professionalism and Scientific Rigor in Public Administration

The public administration literature prominently includes legitimation claims that call for increased professionalization and research-based expertise (Houston & Delevan, 1990; McCurdy & Cleary, 1984; Perry & Kraemer, 1986; Stallings & Ferris, 1988). These legitimation claims are in keeping with the themes of modernity, and they represent an orthodoxy in public administration that became fully visible in the Progressive Era and has continued, albeit with ebbs and flows, to the present.

The calls for increased professionalization are prominently marked by the publication of two full symposia in the

Public Administration Quarterly (Winter, 1985, and Spring, 1986). Although professionalism is most concerned with the *practice* of public administration, it is also of serious concern to academics in the field for reasons spelled out clearly in historical perspective by Larson:

> The unification of training and research in the modern university is a particularly significant development. As graduate and professional schools emerged at the top of the educational hierarchy, the professions acquired not only an institutional basis on which to develop and standardize knowledge and technologies; they also received in university training, a most powerful legitimation for their claims to cognitive and technical superiority and to social and economic benefits. (1977, p. 136)

Of course, public administration is still poorly organized as a profession by comparison with law or medicine, for example, and is unlikely, in the American context where government has consistently been viewed as little better than an unavoidable irritant, to achieve the degree of professionalization to which many in the field clearly aspire.

In the orthodox view, a well-organized academic discipline must have a scientific knowledge base. The calls for greater scientific rigor in public administration follow this credo, which gained ascendancy during the Progressive Era. In spite of acknowledgment of other research traditions, such as the interpretive or critical (White, 1986), this literature judges public administration research according to the "criteria that conventionally define careful systematic study in social science" (McCurdy & Cleary, 1984, p. 50). The text cited in reference to this statement is the well-known volume by Kerlinger, *Foundations of Behavioral Research* (1964). Later, the authors assert (McCurdy & Cleary, 1984, p. 55), "If public administration is to be a mature field of study, we feel it must reach agreement on criteria of this nature." A later article by Perry and Kraemer (1986) examines "How *Public Administration Review* methodologies measure up against mainstream social research" (p. 216). Houston and Delevan (1990) assert, "Sound theory however is developed only through the testing and refinement of empirical propositions derived from theory" (p. 678). They find little evidence of such work in public administration and are troubled by this.

There were alternative research traditions and a variety of versions of epistemology in the Progressive Era, as there were in the 1930s, and as there have been for the last quarter century. The calls for increased professionalism and increased scientific rigor nevertheless echo down through the decades of public administration history. Further discussion of modernity may help in understanding such stubborn persistence.

The Implications of Modernity

Modernity has fostered technical rationality, which is part and parcel of the culture at large. The continuing impact of technical rationality on public administration theory and practice can perhaps be illuminated by a brief example from another literature (Adams & Ingersoll, 1990). Not too long ago, there was much written about the concept of *culture* as it applies to the study of organizations. Culture has been utilized in the study of organizations in ways consistent, for the most part, with technical rationality (Barley, Meyer, & Gash, 1988). That is, rather than attention being focused on culture as the larger context of meaning within which organizations are nested, the focus was quickly narrowed to individual organizations, as if each evolved its own largely idiosyncratic "culture" *de novo*. Very quickly, organizational "culture" became another *technique* for the manager's tool bag, and many companies and agencies set out to reshape their corporate "culture" in much the same way that, say, a strategic plan might be initiated.

What accounts for the degeneration of a rich metaphor (in this case, culture) into a passing managerial fad? How is it that we appear unable to think our way out of modernity sufficiently to produce anything other than ephemeral results? Both the example of the literature on organizational culture and the persistent calls for professionalism and scientific rigor in public administration remind one of *pentimenti*, the products of a long-standing practice of artists. Because canvas and stretcher bars are expensive, it has been a common practice for centuries for artists to paint over their earlier paintings in an effort to save money. Over the years, though, an image—a *pentimento*—from the earlier painting may bleed through what has been painted on top. Likewise, over the years public administration theorists have painted new versions of public administration theories over the old, with the traditionalists (discussed in White & McSwain, 1990), the new public administration, and the interpretive and critical versions all among them. Although each of these versions of public administration is thought of as affording an entirely new view of the field, the old images continue to bleed through. These old images—images of technique and rationality—are deeply woven within modernity, and they are not so easily covered over. Let us now turn to a summary of the implications modernity continues to hold for public administration and for administrative evil.

Public Administration: Past and Future

Modernity exacerbates the question of a legitimate role for public administration within the American state. The tension between a meaningful, democratic politics and an expert, specialized administration, embedded in our nation's founding and intensified greatly by the flowering of technical rationality nearly 100 years ago, remains at the forefront of any possible claim to legitimacy for public administration in the American state. An atemporal public administration has considerable difficulty even addressing this question, because in its very essence it is a historical question.

Attention to public administration's past suggests that the broad parameters of ethical behavior, knowledge, and theory development in our field were established in the Progressive Era. Recent calls for increased professionalism and more scientific and rigorous research echo claims made first nearly a century ago. Thus, although there has been considerable historical scholarship in public administration, the *role* of historical analysis in the field remains highly problematic. Remaining enthralled with modernity, we remain unable to locate ourselves in our present historical circumstances and thus relegate ourselves to issuing "new" calls for science and rigor on into the future.

If critical, historically based studies were in the forefront of public administration research, we could more readily consider questions crucial to the present and future configuration of public administration, and to administrative evil. For example, Bauman (1989) and Rubenstein (1975) advance the notion that the conditions and values of modernity have unleashed the most destructive and dehumanizing forces known in human history. Without mentioning public administration by name, Bauman (1989, pp. 73-77) argues that its core values—the engineering approach to society, the institution of expertise, and the practice of scientific management—are essential components of the Holocaust and other instances of contemporary racism and mass exterminations:

> For these reasons, the exterminatory version of anti-Semitism ought to be seen as a thoroughly modern phenomenon; that is, something which could occur only in an advanced state of modernity. To be effective, modern exterminatory

anti-Semitism had to be married to modern bureaucracy.
(Bauman, 1989, p. 76)

Public administration needs to consider not only that
genocide and other acts of administrative evil required modern organizations but also the extent to which modern public
administration is founded on and sustained by systematic
dehumanization, exploitation, and even extermination. To
the extent that this is true—and we will argue that it is in
part—public administration must remake its ethical foundation into one that unmasks and confronts the reality of
administrative evil.

3

Administrative Evil Unmasked

The Holocaust and Public Administration

> Mass murder demands organization. Repeated killing is
> not a deed, a single act, but an activity with all the distin-
> guishing features of work: a task done methodically,
> according to plan, over time, oriented to a goal, marked
> by bureaucratic efficiency and routine.
> —*Wolfgang Sofsky (1997, p. 111)*

◈ The Holocaust is the signal event in human history
that unmasks the reality of administrative evil. Despite
the fact that a number of prominent authors (e.g., Arendt,
1963; Bauman, 1989; Browning, 1983; Hilberg, 1985, 1989;
Rubenstein, 1975) have documented and discussed the role
of the public service in the destruction of Europe's Jews, little
consideration has been given to the notion that the Holocaust
is directly relevant to the theory and practice of public
administration. This lack of attention to the meaning of the
Holocaust for public administration is characteristic of the
field's lack of historical consciousness and represents a
dangerous gap in the self-understanding of the field, one that

contributes to a blindness to the potential for administrative evil and to the fragility of the field's ethical foundations.

This chapter connects public administration to the Holocaust by demonstrating the centrality of routine administrative processes and the regular civil service to the implementation of the Holocaust. We show that the nature and dynamics of these bureaucratic processes are not unique to Nazi Germany or the Holocaust but instead are entirely consistent with modern organizations and the technical-rational approach to administration. The significance of the connection between the Holocaust and the civil service in Germany is such that responsibility for the event shifts to include not only those who planned and committed overt acts of killing innocent human beings but also routine and seemingly neutral acts of state and municipal authorities and thousands of ordinary public administrators. Indeed, without the full complicity of professional civil servants (and myriad other professionals), it is virtually inconceivable that the mass murder of Europe's Jews could have been accomplished. The centrality of public administrators as perpetrators of the Holocaust requires that we seriously call into question the adequacy of the ethical foundations of modern public administration.

The Holocaust

Prior to World War II, there were more than 9 million Jews living throughout Europe. By the end of the war, approximately two thirds, or nearly 6 million, of them were dead (Berenbaum, 1993; Hilberg, 1985). In Poland and other Eastern European countries, more than 90% of the Jews were annihilated. The vast majority of these people died not as casualties of war but as innocent victims of a massive, deliberate effort by Nazi Germany to rid all of Europe of its Jewish population. In addition to Jews, the Nazis murdered hundreds of thousands of other victims, including homosexuals, the handicapped, Gypsies (*Roma*), and many political prisoners from Russia and other Eastern European countries (Arad, Gutman, & Margaliot, 1981; Breton & Wintrobe, 1986; Browning, 1980; Charney, 1984; Dietrich, 1981; Edelheit & Edelheit, 1991; Fein, 1979; Klee, Dressen, & Riess, 1991; Lael & Marcus, 1984; Lipton, 1986; Weinstein, 1980).

The genocide of the Jews and these other "undesirables" was carried out by several means, the most notorious being the infamous "death camps" of Auschwitz-Birkenau, Belzec, Chelmno, Sobibor, and Treblinka, among others. In these camps, nearly 4 million Jews and thousands of other victims were systematically murdered. Most were gassed with an insecticide (Zyklon-B) in the massive gas chambers, but many others died in transit to the camps, or from starvation, disease, and overwork as slaves in the most inhumane and unsanitary conditions imaginable in these and hundreds of other SS concentration camps.

Another 1.5 to 2 million Jews were executed by mobile killing squads (known as *Einsatzgruppen*) and other military and police death squads. Their job in the early stages of the German conquest of Russia was to round up all the Jews in a town, transport them to a remote location, force them to dig their own mass grave, and then shoot everyone, except those deemed (temporarily) useful as slave laborers (Browning, 1992; Goldhagen, 1996). Hence, most of the victims of these execution squads (and the majority gassed in the death camps) were women, children, and the elderly. The gas chambers and crematoria were subsequently developed as a means of killing without the horrors of mass shootings, and to solve the difficulties of disposing of so many dead bodies.

Historical Interpretations of
the Holocaust and the Role
of Public Administration

Historical interpretations of the Holocaust center on two conceptual frameworks, one *intentional* and the other *functional* (Browning, 1989; Mason, 1981). Both frameworks have important implications for the role of public administration in the Holocaust and what it means for the field today. The intentional interpretation (much like Allison's [1971] Model I or rational actor) centers on understanding the unfolding of events that led to the Holocaust as stemming from Hitler's explicit intention to annihilate the Jews and other "undesirable" peoples. This objective was derived from his racist ideology and was implemented by his henchmen through the deliberate plans and centralized commands of an all-powerful totalitarian dictatorship.

Intentional interpretations of the Holocaust emphasize its uniqueness in history as an unprecedented event, in terms of both its enormous scale and the inhumanity of the killing processes. The physical destruction of Europe's Jews is seen as a fixed goal in Hitler's mind from the beginning. Events that transpired subsequent to that decision were orchestrated steps on the road to realizing this twisted vision. When the circumstances of the war provided the opportunity, Hitler acted to accomplish his goal of annihilating the Jews. The most important of the two decision points is the former, when Hitler decided what must be done. The decisions as to how and where were relatively incidental and entirely consistent with his original vision, which was conceptualized 22 years before its implementation (Dawidowicz, 1975). In this framework, evil stems from Hitler's intent to annihilate the Jews, and the role of public administration in the Holocaust is a secondary one, as civil servants acted as extensions of and in response to the Nazi dictatorship. They were all just following orders.

Functional interpretations of the Holocaust (which include aspects of Allison's [1971] Model II, organizational processes, and Model III, governmental politics) downplay the importance of Hitler's intentions and the role of central planning, emphasizing instead how the "final solution" emerged from the chaotic interplay of changing circumstances, separate and often competing organizational structures, established bureaucratic procedures, and improvised decision processes. This perspective focuses on the somewhat anarchical nature of the Nazi state, its internal competition, and its haphazard decision making, which encouraged continuous improvisation at the local or micro level (Broszat, 1981; Browning, 1989). In contrast to the intentional approach, the role of Hitler and the central Nazi leadership is seen as more of a catalyst for these disparate forces than as that of central planners or controlling decision makers. The Holocaust was implemented by a multipronged operation of a decentralized apparatus or web of organizations that depended on administrative discretion, rather than by a centralized command hierarchy (Hilberg, 1989).

The functional perspective sees no meaningful distinction between the conceptualization and implementation of the "final solution" (Browning, 1989, pp. 98-99): "Participation in the Final Solution did not result so much from explicit orders systematically disseminated, as through self-recruitment by the zealous and ambitious servants of the Third Reich in response to the impulses and hints they perceived emanating from the centers of power." Although Hitler's ideological fixation ensured that a final solution to the Jewish problem would be sought, it did not specify the form it would take. As circumstances changed, so did the definition of the problem and its possible solution. Only after considering and experimenting with a number of definitions of and solutions to the Jewish problem did the "final solution" emerge. Even the infamous death camp at Auschwitz was not created for its ultimate role; it evolved through a succession of purposes (Adam, 1989; Dwork & van Pelt, 1996).

Functionalists (for example, Broszat, 1981; Browning, 1989; Hilberg, 1989) argue that the intent to pursue genocide as the final solution was more latent than manifest until it crystallized in the minds of decision makers as previous solutions—such as ghettoization, deportation, and resettlement—proved increasingly unworkable. That is, genocide as an intentional strategy was reconstructed as decision makers became aware of the path they were following and the consequences of their actions. The conception of total genocide emerged from organizational practice and as such processes as sporadic acts of killing groups of Jews and others (gypsies, homosexuals, handicapped) led to the idea of systematically killing all Jews.

The functionalist emphasis on process tends to highlight not the uniqueness and enormity of the Holocaust but rather micro level processes and the extent to which they reflect much "that is familiar and even commonplace in the context of contemporary institutions and practices" (Hilberg, 1989, p. 119). The Nazi dictatorship, German anti-Semitism, and Hitler's racist ideology represent necessary but not sufficient conditions for the Holocaust to occur (Bauman, 1989). Just as important were latent tendencies toward dehumanization within routine bureaucratic processes, "performed by thousands of functionaries in public offices and private enterprises . . . embedded in habit, routine, and tradition" (Hilberg, 1989, p. 119). Those involved in these processes did not merely respond to the Nazi dictatorship but also provided impetus and direction to the genocide.

Ultimately, however, neither the intentionalist nor the functionalist interpretation of the Holocaust provides, by itself, a satisfactory explanation for what happened. Although we cannot penetrate Hitler's mind or even his conversations with his inner circle of advisers, the actions of the Third Reich during the 1930s do not reflect a consistent intention to commit genocide against Europe's, or even Germany's, Jewish population. Several strategies aimed at removing Jews from German society were tried before circumstances and experience led Hitler and the Third Reich to their final solution to the "Jewish problem." A purely functionalist explanation for the Holocaust tends to marginalize Hitler's intentions and influence on events to an extent that obscures his role in leading Germany toward the final solution (see Friedlander, 1997, pp. 1-6).

Appreciating the contributions of both perspectives contributes to a better understanding of how the Holocaust occurred, not as the result of exclusively intentional or functional processes but as the confluence of historical and political forces, racist ideology and anti-Semitism, organizational competition, and the bureaucratic processes of a highly developed modern society. The combination of planning and opportunism, of tight control and improvisation, of rational preparation and intuitive action, was characteristic of how the Nazis acquired, exercised, and eventually fell from power (Browning, 1989; Yahil, 1990, p. 54).

To the extent that both perspectives, intentional and functional, contribute to understanding the Holocaust, organizational structure and modern bureaucratic processes should comprise at least as much of the overall picture as the intentions and directives of the Nazi dictatorship. Functional processes formed the foundation for the vast and systematic mass killing that defined the Holocaust, and it cannot be understood apart from the role played by such relatively mundane operations. As the following sections will show, bureaucratic procedures carried out by regular civil servants were essential to both the formulation and the implementation of the Holocaust. These activities were not carried out by a few specialized departments but by all the public bureaucracies, national and local. No special agency or commission was created to deal with the "Jewish problem." Existing organizations adapted themselves and contributed to the evolving task of separating Jews from the society of the Third Reich to the point where their destruction became the logical and efficient solution to an administrative problem.

Legalizing Evil: The German Civil Service and the Third Reich

Yahil (1990) identifies three basic tools that Hitler used to establish and maintain his totalitarian state—terror (including the SS and Gestapo), legislation, and propaganda. To these we must add public administration. Hitler used all these simultaneously (and sometimes at odds with each other) to achieve his ends, but no significant action was ever carried out that had not first been legally sanctioned (Rubenstein, 1975; Yahil, 1990). This approach allowed Hitler to justify his actions both to the international community and to Germany's civil service, members of which were essential to administering the Nazi state and the Holocaust. Germany's professional civil servants and the courts probably would have fought against a regime that lacked legal and constitutional legitimacy, as they had done against the 1923 putsch (Brecht, 1944).

Following Hitler's election to the chancellory, the Reichstag passed two key pieces of legislation in the spring of 1933. First, the "Emergency Regulation in Defense of the People and the State" abolished the basic individual rights and legal protections of a democratic society. Second, the "Enabling Act," or "Law for Removing the Distress of People and the Reich," provided the legal instrument to sanction and strengthen his dictatorship. The Enabling Act invested Hitler with direct legislative authority, which he used to pass numerous laws aimed at putting the government fully under the control of the National Socialists (Yahil, 1990, pp. 54-55). It also placed the civil service at the disposal of Hitler's cabinet for whatever it deemed fit to decree. Once Hitler was elected and the Enabling Act passed according to constitutional requirements, civil servants had little choice but to fall in line with the new regime or find themselves at odds with an overwhelming power.

Their professional duty, as they understood it, demanded that they apply decrees issued within the limits of the Enabling Act, whether they personally approved or not. The individual public employee was faced with a limited range of choices. He could (a) withdraw and lose employment, with potentially dire consequences; (b) stay in office and warn or advise during the preparation stages of new measures; or (c) try to undermine the regime. As Brecht (1944) said, "Only someone who is well acquainted with the German civil servants is able to estimate the torment through which many of them have gone since Hitler's access to power" (p. 113). The legalistic measures of the Nazi regime left little opportunity for concerted resistance. Once a decree based on the Enabling Act was issued, civil servants felt obligated to execute measures that fell under their jurisdiction (Brecht, 1944, p. 105).

The importance of a cooperative and dutiful public bureaucracy to the Third Reich is reflected in the fact that the first basic statute passed under the Enabling Act was the "Law for the Restoration of the Professional Civil Service," promulgated on April 7, 1933, together with a statute that restricted the independence of the secondary states in favor of the central government. The intent of this legislation was to remove Jews and other "unreliables" from important government posts (Yahil, 1990, p. 64; see also Browning, 1983), and it represented a key first step in separating Jews from German society. Not all Jews, however, were removed at first. At President Hindenburg's insistence, World War I veterans were retained, and those who were dismissed received their regular pensions. Even "unreliables" received 75% pensions. These were not revoked until the end of 1938 (Brecht, 1944, p. 110).

According to Brecht (1944, pp. 110-111), the majority of dismissals came from the ranks of the higher civil service. Out of 1,663 Prussian members of the higher civil service in field positions, 469, or 28%, either were dismissed as "unreliable" or Jewish (12.5%), or were demoted to lower positions for "administrative reasons" (15.5%). In the middle brackets of the civil service, including the clerical class, only 3.46% were affected (1.13% "unreliable"; 2.33% for "other reasons").

These figures should not lead to the conclusion that most remaining civil servants belonged to the Nazi Party. The great majority did not belong, especially during the 1930s. Most civil servants were neither creations of the Nazi state nor old-fashioned anti-Semites. They were career professionals who valued competence, efficiency, and their ability to overcome obstacles and adverse conditions, and they often knew what to do without asking for direction (Hilberg, 1989, pp. 132-133). They wanted to keep their jobs and were allowed to do so because they were needed to administer the state and their functions were considered politically neutral, constituting no political danger to the rule of National Socialism. Indeed, widespread dismissals would have posed a much greater threat to the regime's stability. The legislative and legalistic measures taken by the new government reassured most civil servants that their actions were legally justifiable and maintained their continued reliability as administrators in nonpolitical posts.

One of the immediate effects of the Law for the Restoration of the Professional Civil Service was that civil servants throughout Germany became deeply involved in the highly bureaucratic process of determining who was or was not a Jew. The law contained the first official definition of a Jew, and genealogical and medical records had to be tracked down and verified for thousands of individuals; that is, for anyone suspected of being Jewish. These investigations led to the dismissals of thousands of Jews from civil service positions, to prohibitions from the practice of law and medicine, and to many other prohibitions and restrictions in all areas of political, social, and cultural affairs (Friedlander, 1997). There is little evidence that government employees objected to these background investigations or questioned the policy of separating Jews from German society.

When viewed as a whole, therefore, there appears to have been very little direct prodding, and certainly no wholesale purging of German public administration (Hilberg, 1989, p. 129). Most civil servants were relatively comfortable in positions that entailed "morally neutral" functions, such as economic affairs, tax collection, social security, statistics, railroad service, foreign currency, and municipal government, meaning that their work could not be implicated directly in acts they would judge to be immoral, illegal, or unethical. Direct acts of murder and cruelty generally were the provenance of the SS and were not assigned to permanent officials. If indirectly involved in such actions, they would try to be "fair" to the victims and attend to the details of administration within the boundaries of the law. Being of such service may have brought some moral conflict to civil servants in the Third Reich, but most reasoned that matters would only be worse if they failed to cooperate and do their duty (Brecht, 1944, p. 106). A closer examination of these so-called morally neutral functions will show that such activities were not as neutral or peripheral to the killing process as civil servants might have liked to believe. As Hilberg (1989, p. 129) points out, they contributed their share to the destruction of the Jews as a matter of course.

Implementing Evil: The German Civil Service and the Holocaust

Most generally, the Holocaust evolved from the efforts of the Nazi state to solve the "Jewish problem," or how to accomplish the separation of the Jews from German society, and eventually from all of Europe. It became, essentially, a vast and complex administrative problem. As the policy evolved, it was up to the various components of the public bureaucracy to figure out how to accomplish it. The difficulty of the problem stemmed from the fact that, anti-Semitism aside, Jews were fully entwined with every aspect of German (and European) society—economic, political, social, and cultural. No matter how virulent Hitler's hatred of the Jews and the zeal of his followers, Jews could not suddenly be exiled or killed without severely disrupting the social fabric and political economy of German society. This was so clear that even Hitler did not pursue such an approach in the early years of his regime (Browning, 1989).

Anti-Jewish legislation of the 1930s reflects the gradual escalation of a policy to remove Jews from German society (Bauman, 1989; Rubenstein, 1975; Yahil, 1990). The denationalization decrees of the 1930s empowered the minister of the interior to cancel naturalization granted since the end of World War I and provided that all German citizens residing outside the Reich could be deprived of their citizenship. The ultimate impact of this decree was felt in 1941, when the Reich Citizenship Law was amended to provide that a Jew "who takes up residence abroad" was no longer a Reich national and that this person's property was to be confiscated by the state. As soon as the Gestapo transported Jews beyond the German border, regardless of their unwillingness to go, they lost all rights as citizens. No government was concerned for their fate, and thus the Nazis had eliminated all legal impediments to carrying out the final solution (Rubenstein, 1975, pp. 32-33). The legal conversion of Jews from citizens into aliens preceded their destruction. Before they were executed, the Jews had ceased to exist as members of a political community.

Before this occurred, the authorities had to deal with the fact that the Jewish communities were entwined with German society. Various measures were needed to sever these connections without violating the rights or interests of the non-Jewish population. The necessary actions to implement anti-Jewish legislation thus had to be taken by technical specialists—accountants, lawyers, engineers, physicians, and others, many of whom belonged to the public service. Many technical and legal issues had to be resolved, such as the following: Who was (or was not) a Jew? What about a mixed marriage? How was a "Jewish enterprise" to be defined? How were their assets to be disbursed? Where were the boundaries of a ghetto to be drawn? These administrative problems were dealt with by bureaucrats in their memoranda, correspondence, meetings, and discussions (Hilberg, 1989, pp. 120-121).

Legal procedures and accounting routines were essential to the process of removing Jews from German society, through a decentralized apparatus that was attempting to preserve non-Jewish rights and to balance the books at all times. By following proper procedures, the German public administrator could feel satisfied that his actions were appropriate and legal. He could separate his actions from their inhuman consequences by equating correctness with rightness, and accuracy with accountability. In this way, the German bureaucracy adapted to the evolution of Nazi anti-Jewish policy from legislative discrimination and expropriation to deportation and extermination (Browning, 1983, p. 147).

Perhaps the most frightening aspect of the Holocaust is that it was accomplished in large part by the public service carrying out routine functions as if virtually nothing was out of the ordinary (Hilberg, 1989): "In the final phases, not even orders were needed. Everyone knew what had to be done, and no one was in doubt about directions and goals. . . . The fact is that the initiators, formulators, and expediters, who at critical junctures moved the bureaucratic apparatus from one point to the next, came from within the apparatus" (p. 128). Understandably, history has focused on the brutality of the SS, the Gestapo, and infamous concentration camp doctors and guards. Much less attention has been given to the thousands of public administrators such as those in the Finance Ministry who engaged in confiscations, the armament inspectors who organized forced labor, or municipal authorities who helped create and maintain ghettos and death camps throughout Germany and Eastern Europe. The destruction of the Jews was procedurally indistinguishable from any other modern organizational process. Great attention was given to precise definition, to detailed regulation, to compliance with the law, and to record keeping. In other words, the modern, technical-rational approach to public administration was adhered to in every aspect.

For example, one difficult administrative problem involved the financing of rail transport, which was essential to the destruction process. Jews were transported out of Germany and other European countries to the death camps, a process that stripped them of all legal protections and allowed the Nazis to execute them away from major population centers. Bureaucratic procedure had to be followed, however, and dictated that no agency, including the Gestapo or the SS, could simply use the trains as they saw fit. The German Rail Authority derived its revenue from individual clients or organizations requiring space on its trains. The client for the trains to the death camps was the Gestapo, and the travelers—one way only—were Jews. The fare, payable by Gestapo offices, was calculated at the passenger rate, third class, for the number of track kilometers, one way only, with discounts for children. Group rates were applied to transports exceeding 400 individuals. For the guards, the round trip fare had to be paid (Hilberg, 1989, pp. 129-131). It was in this routine, matter-of-fact way that whole communities were transported to their deaths.

The Gestapo, however, had no budget for transport, and there was no precedent for simply charging such expenses to the Finance Ministry. The Gestapo solved the problem by developing a "self-financing" scheme that shifted the burden of funding to authorities in the foreign areas where Jewish properties had been expropriated or even to the Jewish communities themselves. Levies were collected and deposited in special accounts "W" which the Gestapo controlled and then paid to the rail authority. The Finance Ministry condoned this practice even though it constituted an evasion of the basic principle that only the ministry could collect funds for the Reich and disburse them to agencies. By allowing the Gestapo to find and implement a creative solution, albeit one of questionable legality, to the financing problem, the basic framework of routine bureaucratic procedures could be preserved, allowing civil servants to focus on their administrative responsibilities with a minimum of disruption or moral discomfort.

The financing of rail transport illustrates the combination of technical-rational administrative procedures with the improvisation and opportunism that characterized the many activities that contributed to the Holocaust. Every effort was made to preserve the facade of legality and proper procedures at all times, and to find the most efficient solution to the problem. The approach was consistently impersonal and dehumanizing. Hilberg points out how this approach is reflected in the reporting system. Offices and field units would make reference to the "final solution" in long summaries of diverse activities, following a rigid format and matter-of-fact style that masked the nature of the activities. "The Jews are absorbed in the daily passage of events, and there is seldom any disconcerting emphasis on their ultimate fate" (Hilberg, 1989, p. 131). Jews basically became a subheading under normal bureaucratic lists of wages, rations, taxes, transport, and other routine matters.

It is important to recognize, however, that the routine duties and procedures carried out by civil servants contributed to the Holocaust—to mass murder—in more direct ways. Concentration and death camps had all the problems of new towns, and they generated externalities that affected the surrounding communities and environment. The SS and Gestapo found that they could not carry out their grim mission without the aid of competent and diligent public administrators. Although the SS had complete control over what happened in camps once they were built, it had to conform to normal planning and inspection procedures while the camps were under construction. Public officials dealt with the siting and maintenance of death camps in much the same way as they would any other public facility or private industry, as illustrated by the following comments by a provincial planner in the Auschwitz region:

> When I gave my permission some time ago to create a concentration camp, I made it clear that a camp of this enormous size, located in such an extraordinarily well-located place for industry . . . would be expected to accept many conditions in the interest of other parties or for the common good. (in van Pelt, 1994, p. 134)

Problems commonly dealt with by public bureaucracies took on horrific and dehumanizing properties in the context of genocide and the Holocaust.

A particularly vexing problem at the larger concentration and death camps involved the processing and disposal of human waste (a separate issue from the disposal of ashes from the crematoriums). The attempt to dispose of waste in the most efficient manner (best results at the least cost) resulted in systems that stripped inmates of the last vestiges of their humanity and wreaked havoc on the surrounding environment and communities (van Pelt, 1994). The initial reluctance of the SS to invest resources and manpower in the construction of adequate latrines and wastewater facilities at Auschwitz resulted in large amounts of sewage flowing into the Vistula river and strained relations with the surrounding communities. By 1943, teams of engineers and planners were fully engaged in designing a sewage treatment facility for Auschwitz. Although none of the civil servants who worked on the sewage problem directly killed anyone, the camp's continued operation required their complicity (van Pelt, 1994, pp. 135-136).

In discussing the role of the railroad administration in the Holocaust, Hilberg points out that its heavy participation in activities that supported the genocide of the Jews should command attention because neither it nor most other public agencies in Nazi Germany conformed to any common definition or characteristics of an ideological vanguard or movement (Hilberg, 1989, p. 126): "If nothing else, their history should tell us that if Hitler and the Nazi Movement . . . were essential for the Holocaust to occur, so was at least in equal measure the readiness of ordinary agencies to engage in extraordinary tasks inherent in the Final Solution."

Does this mean that German public administrators were "willing executioners" (Goldhagen, 1996), or banal functionaries who merely followed orders (Arendt, 1963)? The answer, as in the intentionalist versus functionalist debate, is both. The genocide, both intentional and functional in nature, was not simply the result of carrying out well-defined orders from the center or of spontaneous killing; it evolved through a series of steps, from seeking solutions to successive problems, which included how to get the most slave labor out of prisoners while systematically killing them, how to make the killing easier for the executioners, and how to dispose of the thousands of bodies "produced" by the killing process. The death and slave labor camps, gas chambers, and crematoriums were the final solution to these and other aspects of the "Jewish problem" and were relatively short steps to take after traveling a long road toward this horrific administrative evil (Bauman, 1989; Browning, 1992).

Perfectly Safe Ground?

More than 50 years later, what is the meaning of the Holocaust for public administration and for administrative evil? There is no single, satisfactory answer to this question. Given what we know about the Holocaust and how it happened, however, we would pose an imperative that public administrators (and other professionals) continually raise this question and make it part of the very identity of the field. For example, the role of the professional civil service and public bureaucracy in the Holocaust should give us pause when we consider the following statement by Woodrow Wilson from his classic essay on the study of administration, a work that continues to influence conventional views of public management and administration (see, for example, Lynn, 1996, p. 39).

> When we study the administrative systems of France and Germany, knowing that we are not in search of *political*

principles, we need not care a peppercorn for the constitutional or political reasons which Frenchmen or Germans
give for their practices. . . . If I see a murderous fellow
sharpening a knife cleverly, I can borrow his way of sharpening the knife without borrowing his probable intention to
commit murder with it; and so, if I see a monarchist dyed
in the wool managing a public bureau well, I can learn his
business methods without changing one of my republican
spots. . . . By keeping this distinction in view,—that is, by
studying administration as a means of putting our own
politics into convenient practice . . . we are on perfectly safe
ground. (Wilson, 1887, p. 221)

Wilson wrote at the end of the 19th century and in the
heyday of Progressivism, before the horrors of the world
wars. At the close of the 20th century, it is difficult, standing
in the long shadow of the Holocaust, to conclude that public
administrators, in whatever political context, can find anything resembling safe ground anywhere. The historical record shows that the Holocaust was not the result of a departure from the practice of modern, technical-rational
administration, but instead represents one of its inherent—
and now demonstrated—possibilities (Bauman, 1989;
Rubenstein, 1975). The public service facilitated the killing
process from ghettoization, to deportation, to slave labor and
systematic killing, to the disposal of millions of bodies. As
the "final solution" evolved, there was nothing that is normally considered part of modern public administration—
professional education and expertise, ethical standards, scientific methods, bureaucratic procedures, accountability to
elected officials, and so on—that could prevent or resist the
genocide of the Jews. Public administrators were both willing and helpless in the face of great evil. Today, they remain
just so because administrative evil wears a mask.

Although there is little in the way of solace or comfort to
be found in the history of public administration and the

Holocaust, it does tell us that public administrators—scholars, students, and practitioners alike—would do well to reflect on the possibility that their systems and actions can contribute to the worst kinds of human behavior, and that our ethical standards and professional training do not adequately address the potential for administrative evil. In this era of increasingly ideological and polarized politics (Hunter, 1991; Lowi, 1995) and unwanted, surplus populations (Rubenstein, 1983), public administration should not be taught, practiced, or theorized about without considering the psychological, organizational, and societal dynamics that can lead public servants to confound the public interest with acts of dehumanization and destruction.

4

Administrative Evil Masked

From Mittelbau-Dora and Peenemünde to the Marshall Space Flight Center

> I could not watch the Apollo mission without remember-
> ing that that triumphant walk was made possible by our
> initiation to inconceivable horror.
> —*Jean Michel, Mittelbau-Dora survivor (1979, p. 247)*

◆ In this chapter, we tell the story of the von Braun team of German rocket scientists and engineers who were brought to the United States after World War II. They were to become the premier rocket development team in this country, and in the 1960s, they designed and built the Saturn rockets that propelled Apollo to the moon. Although rumors about their past apparently followed the von Braun team from their first stop at Fort Bliss, Texas, to their eventual American home of Huntsville, Alabama, and the Marshall Space Flight Center, the version of history they told had rather tenuous connections with the administrative evil that dirtied some of their hands and that they tried to leave behind at Peenemünde and Dora.

Of the 118 members of the von Braun team who came to the United States in 1945 (many hundreds of Germans, some connected to von Braun and others not, came later), about half had been members of the Nazi Party; most of these were so-called nominal members and therefore not barred by policy from entering the United States. At least a handful, including Wernher von Braun himself, had been actively engaged first in the decision to use, and then in using, SS-provided slave labor in weapons production, an act that led directly to a war crimes conviction against Albert Speer, Hitler's minister of armaments, among others. In the end, we are left with the reality that a handful of America's most competent and successful public managers in the government agency that was lionized in the 1960s as the paradigmatic high-performing organization either had been "committed Nazis" or had themselves directly engaged in actions for which others in postwar Germany were convicted of war crimes. This story begins at Mittelbau-Dora, where administrative evil wore no mask.

Mittelbau-Dora

Although Mittelbau-Dora was not one of the most notorious concentration camps of the Holocaust, it does merit a special place in the history of the 20th century. Dora was not among the infamous death camps, such as Auschwitz-Birkenau—part of that camp became essentially a factory for killing in which the gas chambers could house 2,000 of the doomed at one time. Rather, Dora was a slave labor camp, and even in this, it was far from unique—large German corporations invested heavily in concentration camp industry, such as IG Farben at Auschwitz. Indeed, Heinrich Himmler, head of the SS, expressly created the "Economic and Administrative Office" for this purpose:

The SS began, in effect, a rent-a-slave service to firms and government enterprises at a typical rate of four marks a day for unskilled workers and six marks for skilled ones. In return, the SS supplied guards, food, clothing, and shelter, usually in a manner that led to a heavy death toll from starvation, disease and overwork. The lives of camp inmates were, by definition, expendable. (Neufeld, 1996, p. 186)

Dora was unique for other reasons.

Mittelbau-Dora was the last SS concentration camp to be established, and it was the only one exclusively formed for the purpose of weapons production. It was one of the first camps liberated by advancing American troops, and some of the first images of corpses stacked like cordwood and the thin ranks of emaciated survivors were from there. Dora was the site of the huge, underground Mittelwerk factory that built the V-2 rockets for the Reich. Mittelwerk produced about 6,000 rockets and 20,000 deaths in its less than 2 years of operation (Neufeld, 1996). Each V-2 rocket thus carried, at least symbolically, three corpses with it to its final destination. During two periods of its short life, it was arguably among the worst of the living hells produced by the SS concentration camps.

Dora was initially a minor appendage of the better known Buchenwald concentration camp. Only in 1943, when Hitler decided to make V-2 rocket production the top armament priority, did Dora mushroom. In August, 1943, after the extensive British air raid on Peenemünde, the Nazi rocket development facility on the Baltic Ocean, V-2 production had to be moved to a place as secure from air attack as possible. An underground location had become the preferred choice for all of German armament and industrial production at this time. The original Nazi plan for the Mittelwerk mining complex near Nordhausen in the province of Thuringia was to house a large petroleum reserve there. Mittelwerk had two huge tunnels, each about a mile in length and each large enough to accommodate two rail lines apiece. These two main tunnels were connected at regular intervals by smaller tunnels of 500 feet apiece; there were 46 of these. All told, Mittelwerk incorporated about 35 million cubic feet of space. At its peak, 10,000 slave laborers at a time lived and toiled in this massive complex.

The Beginning

Unfortunately for those who would work and perish there, SS General Hans Kammler was placed in charge of the construction necessary to make Mittelwerk operational. He had also been in charge of constructing the F-1 production facility at Peenemünde. He was an architect and civil engineer who in 1942 was placed in charge of the SS Economic and Administrative Office. He joined the Nazi Party in 1931 and the SS in 1933. Kammler's resume included the razing of the Warsaw ghetto and the construction of the death camps at Maidenek and Belzec, as well as the later phases of the Auschwitz death camp. He had a well-earned reputation as among the most vicious and inhuman in the entire SS pantheon (Hilberg, 1989).

During the early phase at Mittelwerk, prisoners were housed in several of the cross tunnels, but these were immediately adjacent to the final mining operations in Tunnel A, which was being punched through to the south side of the mountain. This meant that after working 12-hour shifts, prisoners were crammed into bunks (sometimes two at a time) where they could get little or no sleep because of continuous mining noise, including use of explosives.

> In the tunnels of the Mittelwerk, the conditions which were initially intolerable got worse. Two shifts alternated sleeping in bunks, which were stacked four deep. There was no heat,

no ventilation, no sinks, no tubs to bathe in. The food was often soup, usually vile and always insufficient. There was no water. The prisoners found themselves drinking the water that oozed from the rock walls and condensed from the cold, damp air; it collected in muddy puddles on the tunnel floor. The latrines were half barrels with planks laid across their open tops. Not surprisingly, disease ran rampant amid the inescapable filth. Scabies, ulcers, abscesses, gangrene, anemia and dysentery were the common lot. (Piskiewicz, 1995, p. 134)

These conditions led inexorably to remarkable death rates: In October, 1943, 18; in November, 172, in December, 670; in January, 1944, 719, in February, 536, and in March, 767. Until a crematorium could be built at Dora, the dead were stacked at the railhead for shipment to the crematorium at Buchenwald. Dora quickly developed a considerable reputation at Buchenwald. There were also transports of the seriously ill or otherwise "useless" prisoners to death camps such as Bergen-Belsen. Dora's death toll during this early construction phase was estimated at 6,000 in 6 months.

Dr. A. Poschmann, medical supervisor of the Armaments Ministry, visited the Mittelwerk at this time. A few years later at the Nuremburg war crimes trials, he would describe what he had seen, confirming the reports of inmates who had survived. The slaves, Dr. Poschmann said, ". . . worked a minimum of 72 hours a week, they were fed 1,100 calories a day. Lung and heart disease were epidemic because of the dampness and intense air pressure. Deaths averaged 160 a day. When a deputation of prisoners petitioned for improved conditions, SS Brigadefuehrer Hans Kammler responded by turning machine guns on them, killing 80." (Piskiewicz, 1995, p. 135)

As Kammler knew only too well, there was a virtually inexhaustible supply of slave labor available to the SS.

The Mittelwerk Factory

For a 6-month period in 1944, conditions got better—at least, relatively—at the Mittelwerk. SS General Kammler's lowest priority had been the construction of the Dora camp itself, but when this was completed and the 10,000 workers were moved out of the tunnels, sleep became at least a possibility. Now that the factory was primarily devoted to the production of V-2 missiles, workers were somewhat better treated, at least until acts of sabotage and resistance began to appear. The warm weather months helped as well. During this half-year period, the monthly death rate was under 1,000, although this figure does not count transports to death camps of prisoners who were ill or otherwise unable to work.

In September, 1944, the SS formally created Mittelbau-Dora as a separate administrative entity from Buchenwald, the last of the SS concentration camps. At that time, the total camp population was more than 32,000, with nearly 14,000 in Dora itself. Initially, there were few Jews at Dora, unlike most of the other camps. About a quarter of the Dora inmates were Russian, another quarter were Polish, and one seventh were French. There were also about 1,000 Germans, 500 Czechs, and smaller numbers of Gypsies, Belgians, Italians, and Hungarian Jews. The first Jews arrived at Mittelbau-Dora in May, 1944, during the massive transports of Hungarian Jews. The large majority of them went straight to the gas chambers of Auschwitz. Dora was thus unique as well because there were comparatively few Jews in its inmate population. This changed somewhat as the war's end drew nearer.

The Catastrophic End

By the end of 1944 and the first two months of 1945, the inmate population began to grow, and conditions deteriorated quickly. As the Russians advanced from the east, the concentration camps located in Poland began to be overrun, and the SS instituted the practice of shipping the remaining inmates to other camps and then attempting to destroy the camps and with them, the evidence of their horrors. Large numbers of Jews from Auschwitz in particular, but also from Gross Rosen and Mauthausen, were shipped to Mittelbau-Dora, with the overall prisoner population reaching a peak of more than 40,000 and Dora itself housing nearly 20,000.

This period of time also saw the SS response to acts of sabotage and resistance among the Dora inmates. A series of public hangings began, using the large crane (which hoisted the V-2's upright for a final check) in one of Mittelwerk's main tunnels. These escalated when Richard Baer, who had been Auschwitz's last commander, succeeded Otto Forschner as the Mittelbau-Dora commandant (Forschner moved on to Dachau). After a rebellion and breakout of 53 Russian prisoners (nearly all of whom were captured and killed), Baer simply executed all the other Russians and Poles who lived in that particular barracks—nearly 200 prisoners. Production of the V-2 continued into March. In April, 1945, the camp was evacuated, with most prisoners being shipped to Bergen-Belsen, where survivors were liberated. These last, frantic transports were horrific death marches and train rides during which half and more of the prisoners perished. On one of these marches of inmates from Mittelbau-Dora, the SS and Luftwaffe guards herded 1,000 prisoners into a barn at Gardelagen, then set it on fire (Beon, 1997). They shot those who tried to escape.

One of the early visitors to the just liberated Dora happened to be the famous American aviator Charles Lindbergh, who wrote the following:

"Twenty-five thousand in a year and a half," he said. He was seventeen years old, Polish. . . . "Twenty-five thousand in a year and a half. And from each there is only so much." The boy cupped his hands together to show the measure. I followed his glance downward. We were standing at the edge of what had once been a large pit, about eight feet long, six feet wide, and I guessed at six feet deep. It was filled to the overflowing with ashes from the furnaces—small chips of human bone—nothing else. Apparently bucketsful had been thrown from a distance, as one might get rid of the ashes in a coal scuttle on a rainy day. (Lindbergh, 1978, pp. 348-349)

Of the 60,000 prisoners who went to Mittelbau-Dora, approximately 20,000 perished, more than three for every rocket. About 10,000 of those died directly from work on the V-2. The V-2 was thus a highly unusual weapon:

More people died producing it than died from being hit by it. In round numbers, 5,000 people were killed by the 3,200 V-2s that the Germans fired at English and Continental targets. . . . By that measure, at least two-thirds of all Allied victims of the ballistic missile came from the people who produced it, rather than from those who endured its descent. (Neufeld, 1996, p. 264)

This result was not what the German rocket scientists and engineers, who worked diligently during the war years at a weapons development and production facility on the Baltic coast, had in mind.

Peenemünde

The origins of the German rocket program were in the early 1930s. Although the Luftwaffe (the German air force) would also become interested in rockets, it was army ordnance officers, Karl Becker and Walter Dornberger, who saw in the rocket a potentially fearsome weapon and, also important, a weapon system not banned by the Treaty of Versailles, which ended World War I. Dornberger discovered the young Wernher von Braun, who became one of the world's pioneers of rocket science. Von Braun was born in 1912, the second of three sons of Baron Magnus von Braun and his wife Emmy. At the age of 18, von Braun graduated from high school and enrolled in the Charlottenburg Institute of Technology. He became active in the *Verein fur Raumschiffarhrt* (VfR—Society for Space Travel), which was essentially a rocket club. The club and von Braun attracted Dornberger's attention.

Sufficiently impressed with von Braun's talents, Dornberger made him a civilian employee of the army and financed his education, including the completion of his undergraduate degree and his PhD in physics from the University of Berlin, which he completed in 1934 in a remarkable 2 years. In the mid-1930s, von Braun and a staff of 80 worked on rocket development at Kummersdorf West, near Berlin, which was Germany's first facility for the development of rocketry.

In 1937, the new rocket development facility, *Heeresversuchsstelle* (Army Research Station) Peenemünde, opened, and the entire team moved north to the Baltic coast (Garlinski, 1978; Kennedy, 1983; Klee & Merk, 1965). It was there that the design and testing of the V-1 cruise missile and V-2 rocket were accomplished. Many other projects were pursued during Peenemünde's 8-year life. Among them was the conceptual design of an Intercontinental Ballistic Missile (ICBM), which included the calculation of distance trajectories for New York, Pittsburgh, and Washington. Dornberger, who was to become a major general by the end of the war, commanded the facility, and von Braun was the technical director. The group of engineers and scientists, later to be known as the von Braun team and who would follow von Braun to the United States, was first assembled at Peenemünde.

As the rockets grew more successful and the Luftwaffe began to lose effectiveness through continual attrition, attention at Peenemünde began to shift from development to production. As early as 1939, Dornberger had insisted that Peenemünde must incorporate full production facilities on site, and this was in fact accomplished by 1941. Further production facilities were secured in the following 2 years, including Friedrichshafen on Lake Constance near Switzerland, Wiener-Neustadt in Austria, and Zement in Czechoslovakia. The first V-2 (or A-4, as it was known in Peenemünde) launch was in 1942, but numerous problems delayed its readiness for full production. The "A-4 Special Committee" was formed to ensure that full production could get under way when the rocket was ready. The Peenemünde production facilities had used prisoner of war (POW) labor from two camps in the immediate area, Karlshagen and Trassenheide. These prisoners were primarily Polish and Russian POWs. Ironically, the bulk of the casualties of the initial British air raid on Peenemünde in August, 1943, were in these two camps, which had no underground bunkers as protection against air raids. In a further irony, it was two Polish POWs from the Trassenheide camp who got word through the resistance to the British about the existence of Peenemünde; they perished in the air raid.

Throughout German industry from 1941 on, there were increasingly severe labor shortages. The Russian front demanded more and more manpower for the German army. In such difficult circumstances, the use of POW forced labor, although lamentable, seems predictable enough. This was the initial choice at Peenemünde for rocket production. The use of slave labor was an entirely different issue. These were concentration camp prisoners (Häftlinge) under the control of the SS. Wernher von Braun was fully aware during this time of the use of SS-provided slave labor in the production of rockets; indeed, the management team led by Dornberger and von Braun explicitly discussed and adopted as policy the use of SS-provided slave labor in rocket production (Neufeld, 1996, p. 187). Slave labor had been investigated, promoted, and then requisitioned by Arthur Rudolph:

> Slave laborers not only worked at Peenemünde, they were requisitioned from the SS by the army's rocket development group. In a note dated April 16, 1943, Arthur Rudolph, who headed the Development and Fabrication Laboratory, reported on his observations of the exploitation of prisoners at the Heinkel aircraft works in Oranienburg. He wrote, "The employment of detainees (Häftlinge) in general has had considerable advantages over the earlier employment of foreigners, especially because all non-work-related tasks are taken over by the SS and the detainees offer greater protection for security." Rudolph concluded, "Production in the F-1 (the main assembly building in Peenemünde) can be carried out by detainees." On June 2, 1943, Rudolph formally requested 1,400 slave laborers from the SS. The first 200 members of this group arrived on June 17. (Piskiewicz, 1995, pp. 96-97)

Based on this policy decision, slave labor was also requisitioned for the other V-2 production facilities at Friedrichshafen, Wiener Neustadt, and, later, at Zement. Walter Dornberger was fully aware of this decision:

> Dornberger's minutes from August 4 read: "As a basic principle, production in all four assembly plants will be carried out by convicts." . . . Rocket assembly would be done primarily by slave labor, a concept Dornberger fully accepted. In a draft of a letter to Saur that he wrote in advance of the meeting, he said: "Production by convicts no objections." To him they were merely factors of production. (Neufeld, 1996, p. 195)

Later, after V-2 production was shifted to Mittelwerk, Dornberger, Rudolph, and von Braun were all present at a May,

1944, meeting in which the use of additional slave labor because of labor shortages was discussed and agreed upon. Wernher von Braun traveled a number of times from Peenemünde to Mittelwerk, as did Dornberger and other members of the von Braun team. Arthur Rudolph was among a number of personnel who moved full-time to Mittelwerk; he became the chief production engineer, with an office on one of the main tunnels. Magnus von Braun, Wernher's brother, worked under Rudolph on site. Another dozen members of the von Braun team who eventually came to the United States also staffed Mittelwerk. No one could have any illusions about a factory whose production mode during most of its existence was quite simply to work its labor force to death, although their roles may not have involved some of them directly in decisions about, or relationships with, Häftlinge. Von Braun's substantial involvement, however, is quite clear:

> There is no doubt that he remained deeply involved with the concentration camps. On August 15, 1944, he wrote to Sawatski (director of Mittelwerk) regarding a special laboratory he wanted to set up in the tunnels. . . . The letter begins:
>
> During my last visit to the Mittelwerk, you proposed to me that we use the good technical education of detainees available to you and Buchenwald to tackle . . . additional development jobs. You mentioned in particular a detainee working until now in your mixing device quality control, who was a French physics professor and who is especially qualified for the technical direction of such a workshop.
>
> I immediately looked into your proposal by going to Buchenwald, together with Dr. Simon, to seek out more qualified detainees. I have arranged their transfer to the Mittelwerk with Colonel Pister (Buchenwald camp commandant), as per your proposal. (Neufeld, 1996, p. 228)

The coming end of the war brought disaster to Mittelbau-Dora, as we have seen, but it was to become a new beginning for the von Braun team of rocket scientists and engineers.

Operations Overcast and Paperclip

The von Braun team was brought to the United States as a part of Operations Overcast and Paperclip (Bower, 1987; Hunt, 1991; Irving, 1965; Lasby, 1971; McGovern, 1964; Simpson, 1988; Stuhlinger & Ordway, 1994). How this happened has two rather distinct story lines. Wernher von Braun clearly relished telling one version of this story; it appears in several publications, most of them sanctioned by NASA or penned by members of the von Braun team. This "official version" usually follows a story line much like this:

> Knowing that Germany was doomed, von Braun, upon arriving back at Peenemünde, immediately assembled his rocket team and asked them to decide to whom did they want to surrender. The Russians frightened most of the scientists; the French would treat them like slaves; the British did not have enough money for a rocket program; that left the Americans. After stealing a train with forged papers, von Braun led 500 people through war-torn Germany to surrender to the Americans. Additionally, the SS had orders to kill the German engineers who built the V-2. Hiding their notes in a mine shaft, the German scientists evaded their own army searching for the Americans. Finally, the entire German rocket team found an American private and surrendered to him. The Americans immediately went to Peenemünde and Nordhausen and captured all of the remaining V-2s and V-2 parts before the Russians. After they had picked the places clean, the American Army destroyed both places with explosives, leaving the remains to the Russians. The Americans brought over 300 train car loads

of spare V-2 parts to the United States. (Graham, 1995, pp. 159-160)

This "official story" has some tenuous connections to what actually happened; in this, it is much like virtually all the von Braun team's disingenuous and self-serving accounts of their wartime experiences.

In January, 1945, both the Russians from the east and the Allies from the west were advancing well into the German homeland. There was considerable confusion, with many parties issuing orders. Military commanders closest to Peenemünde issued orders to remain and defend the home-land. Two engineers who attempted to flee were captured and shot (this appears to be the source of the "order" to shoot the engineers who built the V-2). It was precisely an SS order, however, from none other than General Hans Kammler, that von Braun and his team followed.

It also was a much smaller group, about 10, that decided that the Americans were the best bet, but this decision was not made until months later. Kammler's order was to move nearly all Peenemünde operations—personnel and records—to the Mittelwerk. This is where von Braun and his team spent nearly 3 months. Mittelwerk was still in full produc-tion at this time, and conditions were deteriorating. The thousands of Peenemünde personnel did not all move at once, but over a period of about a month. Of more than 4,000, about three quarters relocated to the Mittelwerk. The Peenemünde records were deliberately hidden in a deserted mine shaft in the area, for use as a bargaining chip with the Americans. As it happened, the rocketeers had no need for such a bargaining chip.

In April, 1945, Kammler issued another evacuation order; this time, the von Braun team was ordered to move to Oberammergau, a small village in the Bavarian mountains of southern Germany. Of the 3,000 who had moved to the

Mittelwerk, only 400 went to Bavaria. One can speculate that von Braun and the others may have welcomed this order, because it had the effect of putting considerable distance between the von Braun team and Mittelwerk and the Dora Camp. Within a week of von Braun's departure, Mittelbau-Dora and the Mittelwerk were liberated by the U.S. Third Army. The von Braun team made contact with the Americans on May 2, 1945. The unconditional surrender of Germany came 5 days later.

Postwar Chaos

The summer of 1945 was chaotic in postwar Germany. Living conditions for ordinary Germans were very difficult. A number of displaced persons (DP) camps had been established for Holocaust survivors and many others who had been imprisoned or otherwise displaced by the Nazis. Conditions in these camps, though an infinite improvement over concentration camps, were also difficult. As the war was winding down, a large number of technical teams were formed under the auspices of the Combined Intelligence Objectives Committee (CIOS); these teams had a three part-mission:

> First, they were to find out what the Germans knew about weapons, radar, synthetic rubber, torpedoes, rockets, jet engines, infrared, communications, and other such things. . . . Secondly, they were to gather information that could help shorten the war against Japan. . . . Finally, the CIOS teams were to locate and detain—even intern—German scientists and technicians to interrogate them for information . . . and to prevent them from slipping away to seek safe haven in another country and continue their wartime research and development programs and projects. (Gimbel, 1986, p. 436)

These CIOS technical teams represented a developing U.S. policy toward German scientific and technical knowledge in the postwar world. This emerging policy was, unsurprisingly in wartime, being handled under the jurisdiction of the U.S. military, in particular, the Joint Chiefs of Staff. Several principles were being advocated, some in at least partial conflict with others. One was not to repeat the mistake of leaving the German nation with the scientific and technical capacity to rearm, as was done after World War I. This principle was given added weight by the demonstrated Nazi superiority in several areas, including rocketry. Another principle was to prevent any intact groups of scientists or technicians from escaping to another country and simply continuing their research. The focus here was primarily on South America, already known to be a destination of choice for escaping Nazis. The principle that became paramount, at least after the fact, was the idea of denying this expertise to our Cold War adversary-to-be, Russia.

Denazification

At the same time, we also had a policy of denazification and of bringing Nazi war criminals to justice (Lippman, 1995; Nolan, 1994). The Joint Chiefs of Staff addressed denazification in Paragraph Six of Directive 1067:

> All members of the Nazi Party who have been more than nominal participants in its activities, all active supporters of Nazism or militarism and all other persons hostile to Allied purposes will be removed and excluded from public office and from positions of importance in quasi-public and private enterprises. . . . Persons are to be treated as more than nominal participants in Party activities and as active supporters of Nazism or militarism when they have (1) held office or otherwise been active at any level from local to national in the party . . . (2) authorized or participated affirmatively in any Nazi crimes, racial persecution or discriminations. . . . No such persons shall be retained in any of the categories of employment listed above because of adminis-

trative necessity, convenience or expediency. (FitzGibbon, 1969, pp. 75-77)

Denazification was carried out first by the military government until May, 1946, and then under the German Law for Liberation from National Socialism and Militarism (Gimbel, 1990, p. 443). The earliest definition of a "committed Nazi" (that is, more than a "nominal Nazi") came in 1944, and included anyone who joined the Nazi Party before Hitler came to power in 1933. A July, 1945, policy listed 136 mandatory removal and exclusion categories, and indicated that Nazi Party membership prior to May, 1937, was cause for mandatory removal and exclusion. The centerpiece for denazification policy was a questionnaire, *Fragebogen*, which was quite widely distributed. Later, when denazification had been turned over to the German authorities, a new questionnaire (*Meldebogen*) was used, and officials utilized five categories for respondents: major offenders, offenders, lesser offenders, followers or nominal Nazis, and persons exonerated. Denazification policy under the Germans became progressively weaker, and after 1948, only the more obvious cases were pursued.

One of the more revealing juxtapositions of these competing U.S. policies thus became evident in and around Mittelwerk and Dora. While two of the CIOS technical teams were rounding up all the V-2 components from the Mittelwerk and interviewing people to find the rocket scientists and engineers, other teams were interviewing Dora survivors and others for the coming war crimes trials and as part of the larger effort at denazification. In a number of instances, these teams were directed to the same people.

Certainly, war criminals and committed Nazis were not going to be welcome in the United States. During the war, the OSS (Office of Strategic Services, the precursor to the CIA) had actively recruited SS and other Germans as intelligence agents—American spies. When OSS director William Sullivan asked President Roosevelt in December, 1944, if these agents could be permitted to enter the United States after the war, his reply was,

> I do not believe that we should offer any guarantees of protection in the post-hostilities period to Germans who are working for your organization. I think that the carrying out of any such guarantees would be difficult and probably be widely misunderstood both in this country and abroad. We may expect that the number of Germans who are anxious to save their skins and property will rapidly increase. Among them may be some who should properly be tried for war crimes or at least arrested for active participation in Nazi activities. Even with the necessary controls you mention, I am not prepared to authorize the giving of guarantees. (Hunt, 1991, p. 10)

We will, of course, never know whether Roosevelt might have had a different answer for German scientists and engineers needed by this country to achieve technological superiority.

As noted, two of the CIOS technical teams were targeted at the Peenemünders, because the chief of the Rocket Branch in the Ordnance Department at the Pentagon was very interested in the V-2 rocket. It was well known that the Germans had advanced rocketry, far beyond that of either the Americans or the Russians. Colonel Holger Toftoy was in charge of the two Army Ordnance technical teams in Europe. One team focused on locating and interrogating rocket personnel and was headed by Major Robert Staver. Wernher von Braun, regarded as the world's premier rocket scientist, was at the top of his list. In the summer of 1945, some 400 rocket scientists and engineers from Peenemünde and Mittelwerk were gathered in Garmisch-Partenkirchen for interrogation. Soon, Operations Overcast and Paperclip would bring hundreds of German scientists, engineers, and technical experts to the United States. The actual task of moving all the available V-2 rockets and spare parts fell to the second technical team, headed by Major James Hamill. His team essentially cleaned out the Mittelwerk (which was located in the soon-to-be Russian zone) and shipped everything possible by rail to Antwerp in Belgium, where it filled 16 Liberty Ships, for passage to the United States.

In August, 1945, the United States initiated Operation Overcast, the aim of which was to bring selected Germans to this country to participate in the production of German-inspired weapons, including V-2s, against the Japanese. Overcast was given final approval in August, 1945; the Japanese surrendered later that month. Overcast included an assurance that if any committed Nazis were inadvertently brought to the United States, they would be returned to Europe for trial.

In September, 1945, Wernher von Braun and 118 members of the von Braun team came to the United States under Operation Overcast, which was revised and renamed Operation Paperclip in March, 1946. Under Overcast, Colonel Toftoy had succeeded in obtaining early permission to bring over this key group of rocket scientists and engineers. Their first stops were Fort Bliss, Texas, and the nearby White Sands, New Mexico, proving grounds, where they supervised a large number of V-2 launches. By the end of the 1940s, they moved on to the Redstone Arsenal at Huntsville, Alabama, which later became the Marshall Space Flight Center.

Although Paperclip was publicly announced as over in 1952, it apparently continued covertly at least until 1973 (Hunt, 1991). The Paperclip policy, as proposed by Secretary of State Acheson and approved by President Truman, expanded the number of German personnel that could be brought to the United States up to 1,000:

The specialists would be under military custody, since they would enter the United States without visas. The War Department would screen their backgrounds and assure that "the best possible information" about their qualifications was submitted to the State and Justice Departments for visa consideration. Employment contracts would provide for their return to Germany if they were found not to be qualified or acceptable for permanent residence. While war criminals were obviously excluded, one clause in the policy banned those active in nazism or militarism as well: "No person found by the commanding general . . . to have been a member of the Nazi party and more than a nominal participant in its activities, or an active supporter of Nazism or militarism shall be brought to the U.S. hereunder." (Hunt, 1991, p. 39)

The impetus for Operation Paperclip was clearly from the War Department. As it happened, the State Department, which was responsible for approving the Germans' entry into the United States and ultimately for granting citizenship, created numerous obstacles for Paperclip:

In the state department, Spruille Braden, the assistant secretary of state for American republic affairs, protested to Acheson that Project Paperclip would permit military research by Germans in this country which they were prohibited by Allied Control Council (ACC) Law No. 25 from doing in Germany. (Gimbel, 1990, p. 44)

Subsequently, the State Department kicked back the first 10 dossiers submitted for visas for Germans who were already in the United States, signalling its intent to require extensive documentation and investigation of these specialists. State Department recalcitrance and other complicating factors eventually caused changes in Paperclip policies.

One of these factors was the fact that a number of Paperclip candidates in Germany were refusing to sign contracts until their future status was clarified. The other, more difficult factor was that some of the von Braun team (and some others) who were in the United States under Overcast contracts that were due to expire in September, 1946, were threatening not to renew their contracts unless their families could join them and unless their status was clarified. The real difficulty was that the Overcast group could not easily be allowed to leave the United States because they already were privy to top secret knowledge about the projects they had been working on.

Thus, the original, practical goals of obtaining as much scientific and technical personnel and information as possible for national security purposes simply superseded other considerations, including legal and ethical ones. What broke the Paperclip logjam was the eventual shift of emphasis away from whether denazification procedures had been followed and toward the satisfaction of two new criteria: whether the individual's entry was in the national interest, and whether the individual was likely to become a security threat to the United States in the future. Michael Neufeld (1996) notes that:

> Security reports for a number of individuals, including von Braun, had to be revised or fudged to circumvent the restrictions that still existed. Some writers have seen those actions as evidence of a conspiracy in the Pentagon to violate a policy signed by President Harry Truman, but it really reflected a conscious choice by the U.S. government, approved up to the level of the Cabinet at least, to put expediency above principle. The Cold War provided ample opportunity after 1947 to rationalize that policy on anti-Communist grounds, but the circumvention of restrictions on Nazis and war criminals would have gone ahead at some level anyway, because the German's technical expertise was seen as indispensable. (p. 271)

Gimbel summarizes the outcome of the shifts in Paperclip policy as follows:

There is no question that the using agencies portrayed their candidates in the best possible light. Engaging in practices that should hardly be a surprise to academicians familiar with personnel evaluations for purposes of reappointment, tenure and promotion, they dissembled, equivocated, fudged and cheated to accomplish their purposes. But they also made effective use of the shift in policy: the shift from consideration of the candidates' activities under the Nazi regime to judgments about their value to the United States and whether their presence constituted a threat to national security. (1990, pp. 462-463)

Von Braun's mentor and boss, Walter Dornberger, was not one of those brought over with the von Braun team. As it happened, the British wanted Dornberger as a potential war criminal, because they had been the primary target of the V-2 missiles. After holding Dornberger in custody for nearly 2 years, until 1947, the British released him when they realized that trying someone responsible for so few deaths—at least relatively speaking—probably was not feasible. Still, he had made an impression on the British (Neufeld, 1996, p. 269): "According to a U.K. interrogator, the former rocket general had 'extreme views' on German domination, and wishes for a Third World War."

Dornberger was brought to the United States immediately thereafter by the Air Force under Operation Paperclip to work as a consultant at Wright Field in Ohio on missiles. He subsequently applied for U.S. citizenship, which he received. In 1950, he took a position with Bell Aerospace Corporation of Buffalo, New York, where he spent the remainder of his career. He rose to become vice president and chief scientist for Bell, and he retired in 1965. He never forgot his protégé, von Braun, and wrote the following for a von Braun *Festschrift*, published in 1963:

Dr. von Braun is a unique person with outstanding ability. I doubt that one could find in the world another human being of the same ability in his field. It is my opinion that he is the first representative of a totally new class of modern creative man, combining in one person outstanding qualities of the scientist, the engineer, the manager, and the true leader. (Stuhlinger, Ordway, McCall, & Bucker, 1963, p. 364)

If the last sentence of the above quotation appears to resonate with the philosophy of Nazism, perhaps that is because Dornberger, although a member of the regular army officer corps, was also a committed Nazi:

In his notebooks one can find a draft of the pep talk he gave to his senior subordinates on assuming the commander's post on May 12, 1942. He states: "My National Socialist beliefs should be widely known." He goes on to say that his sole aim was to, "... put in the hands of the Führer sufficient numbers of this weapon [the A-4, or V-2], which—it is my conviction and unshakable belief—will decide the war." (Neufeld, 1996, pp. 182-183)

Dornberger, who achieved great success as a manager both in Nazi Germany and in the United States, died in West Germany in 1980.

The von Braun Team

Within a few years of the end of World War II, the uncomfortable moments for the von Braun team had largely passed. The U.S. Army clearly had a vested interest in them and had shielded a few of them from having to testify at the Mittelbau-Dora war crimes trial, held at Dachau in 1947. Von Braun himself and other members of the team successfully maintained the fiction that the use of slave labor had been the exclusive province of the SS, and that they were rocket scientists interested in space flight who had been forced to take a temporary detour into wartime weapons development on the way to their real goal. They enjoyed a better than half-hearted acceptance, after a time, by their adopted community of Huntsville, Alabama, and their colleagues within NASA. Still later, they were rewarded for their great achievements in the Apollo program. Huntsville now has a Wernher von Braun civic center, and several of the Germans, including Arthur Rudolph, received NASA's highest civilian honor, the Distinguished Service Award.

Although there were always stories and rumors about the pasts of some members of the von Braun team, it was only after most of them had left government service in the early 1970s that the facts about their past began to emerge. Survivors of the French Resistance who had been imprisoned at Dora knew and spoke the truth all along (Michel, 1979). Americans were much slower to recognize the unsavory pasts of some of these Germans. Still, based on the information we now have, it would be equally mistaken to issue a blanket condemnation of all the Germans who came over with von Braun. Of the 118 who originally came with von Braun, somewhere between half and three quarters had been members of the Nazi Party (Piskiewicz, 1995). Certainly, most of these were only nominal members. Most also had no direct involvement with slave labor and the policy decision to use it. Only four were known to have joined the SS, although there may have been more (Neufeld, 1996). Von Braun himself was one of these, receiving his commission in 1941, although this is not an early membership that ordinarily would mark a "committed Nazi." He is reported to have worn his SS uniform only once; however, it was clearly to his advantage to do so on the day that Heinrich Himmler, the head of the SS, visited Peenemünde to see for himself how rocket development was going. Himmler rewarded von Braun with a promotion to major. In this action and in many others, von Braun appears as more an opportunist than a Nazi. Another SS member was Kurt Debus, an earlier adherent and apparently more committed. Debus reportedly wore his SS uniform regularly at Peenemünde and at one point denounced a colleague as an anti-Nazi to the Gestapo (Piskiewicz, 1995, p. 237). Debus, after working for some time with von Braun in Huntsville, became the first director of the Kennedy Space Flight Center in Florida. Arthur Rudolph was a seriously committed Nazi who joined the party in June, 1931, and who had other early Nazi affiliations as well.

Huntsville, Redstone, and the Marshall Space Flight Center

By 1950, the von Braun team had moved from Texas to Huntsville, Alabama. Although their condition as "prisoners of peace" had already eased somewhat at Fort Bliss, the move to Alabama marked the real beginning of their new American life. The facility in Huntsville that would become the Marshall Space Flight Center was an arsenal developed during World War II as part of the American war effort. After the war, production was shut down and the site was slated for closure. The Army was looking for a facility to house its budding missile program, however, and thus the Redstone Arsenal came into being. From 1950 to 1960, the Redstone Arsenal was the home of the Army Ballistic Missile Agency (ABMA). The ABMA facility at Redstone was run by von Braun and staffed by members of his team.

The 1950s was a decade in which the United States pursued both military ballistic missile development and space applications for those missiles. The Air Force took the lead in ballistic missile development, while the Navy and the Army had competing satellite programs. The Navy's

Vanguard project was given the nod to launch America's first satellite into space. Apparently, this was in part because President Eisenhower balked at the idea of having the Army's team of German rocket scientists be responsible for the first American satellite. When the Navy program sputtered and failed, however, and the Russians successfully launched Sputnik in 1957, the United States turned to the von Braun team, and Explorer was successfully launched by them in 1958. The von Braun team thereby established itself as the premier rocket team in the United States, and it would remain so through the coming decade of space exploration.

NASA was created legislatively in 1958, and the ABMA was one of several agencies transferred over to it as NASA became operational in 1959-1960. The Marshall Space Flight Center was created in 1960, and Wernher von Braun became its first director. The German team formed at Peenemünde had developed the "everything under one roof" approach to rocket development. As it turned out, this approach—having all the scientific and technical expertise for all the subsystems in one location—was consistent with the existing approach in the Army's arsenals:

> At Huntsville, one of the keys to the Germans' success was the "everything-under-one-roof" approach developed at Kummersdorf and Peenemünde under the direction of Becker and Dornberger. It proved very compatible with the U.S. Army's "arsenal system" of in-house development. Under von Braun's leadership, the German-dominated group successfully developed the nuclear-tipped Redstone and Jupiter missiles in the 1950s. The Redstone—which was really just a much-improved A-4 [V-2]—then became the vehicle that put the first American satellite and first American man into space. Finally, under NASA aegis after 1960, the Peenemünders crowned their success with the phenomenally reliable Saturn vehicles, which launched Apollo spacecraft into orbit and put humans on the moon. (Neufeld, 1996, p. 271)

Saturn and Apollo

NASA was widely regarded in the 1960s as the paradigmatic example of the successful, high-performing organization, especially so for a public sector organization (McCurdy, 1993, p. 2; see also Anna, 1976; Delbecq & Filley, 1974; Levine, 1982). The Apollo program and its great success, punctuated by the moon landing, was clearly the principal reason. The von Braun Team at the Marshall Space Flight Center was an integral part of this success; it was their Saturn rockets that boosted all the crews into orbit and on to the moon. The management strategy first developed by von Braun at Peenemünde worked exceptionally well first at Redstone and then at Marshall. As NASA grew at a very rapid pace, and as more and more work was contracted out, it became impossible to retain the "everything under one roof" approach, but von Braun surrendered this ground slowly and never eliminated the philosophy altogether.

For example, Marshall itself actually built the first of the Saturn I vehicles as well as the first few Saturn I-C first stages (Bilstein, 1980). Although they did not construct subsequent versions of the Saturn, they doggedly maintained the in-house technical expertise to duplicate component testing and even some of the hardware. They thus had the technical expertise to understand from the inside out exactly how prime contractors were designing and building the rockets, and thus to see behind unacceptable design compromises. Von Braun described this approach as follows:

> At Marshall we still can carry an idea for a space-launch vehicle and its guidance system from the concept through the entire development cycle of design, development, fabrication and static testing; we have every intention to preserve and nurture a limited in-house capability. . . . In order for us to use the best possible judgment in spending the taxpayer's money intelligently, we just have to do a certain

amount of this research and development work ourselves. We have to keep our own hands dirty to command the professional respect of the contractor personnel. (von Braun, 1963, p. 250)

The von Braun team's philosophy of management was widely known as the "dirty hands" approach. Whether this was some sort of "Freudian slip" concerning their past practices at the Mittelwerk and Peenemünde is unknown, but at a minimum, the irony is striking.

The project manager in charge of the Saturn V Program Office was none other than Arthur Rudolph. Much as von Braun established himself as an outstanding manager and leader in the United States, Rudolph demonstrated outstanding management with the Saturn Program Office. He developed the concept of the "program control center" (PCC), which essentially gathered relevant information about all the Saturn subsystems in one large conference room and made them visually accessible. The Saturn Program Office was typically portrayed as a premier example of the matrix and project forms of management that NASA was nationally famous for during this period:

> The extraordinary success of . . . [NASA] in leading the United States from a position of relative inferiority to one of world leadership in astronautics during the 1960s has stimulated wide interest in the organizational and management systems which contributed to this feat . . . especially project management, because of the public visibility of its projects [including] the moon landing. (Chapman, 1973, p. vii)

James Webb, the NASA administrator during the Apollo years, was given a tour and briefing on the PCC in 1965; he was very impressed: "I saw here . . . one of the most sophisticated forms of organized human effort that I have ever seen anywhere" (Bilstein, 1980, p. 291). The Saturn Program Office was used as a model for the Apollo Program Office at NASA headquarters in Washington, as well as for other NASA centers and for prime contractors. Webb was so impressed that he sent a procession of academics and executives from business and government to Huntsville to see the operation that Rudolph put together (Bilstein, 1980, p. 291).

A look at the organization chart from the Marshall Space Flight Center from 1960 shows that about three quarters of the management and laboratory director positions were held by former Peenemünders. This remained the case during the entire 10-year tenure of von Braun at Marshall. The von Braun team was obviously a very tightly knit group, and it makes sense that they would be, if for no other reason than they came as a group to a new country. They also shared a past, part of which needed to be kept secret. Although most of them were no more than nominal Nazis, and most had not engaged directly in utilizing slave labor or other SS-related activities, their leader and several of the other key members of the team had a past that needed to be hidden—or at a minimum, whitewashed—for the group to be successful in their new country. Keeping this secret, which required widespread collusion, was clearly another factor in the Germans' insularity.

The von Braun team and Marshall actually developed a kind of siege mentality and a feeling that they had to do better work than anyone else to overcome what they perceived as unfair treatment (Piskiewicz, 1995). The von Braun team knew that President Eisenhower had chosen the Navy rocket program to launch America's first satellite, and they knew it was because the Army missile program was run by a "bunch of Germans." The von Braun team felt misunderstood, slighted, and even attacked; quite naturally, they fostered a kind of "fortress Marshall" mentality over the years. Even in the glory years of Apollo, they never felt they received the degree of credit they were due, and all because they were Germans. The organizational culture developed first at Redstone and then at Marshall was thus a defensive one. Their "dirty hands" approach to management, apart from both its logic and its success, was at least in part a manifestation of their need to maintain a kind of "deep control" (McCurdy, 1993, p. 19) over all aspects of their programs—as well as their past.

The hold of the von Braun team over Marshall caused some misunderstanding and resentment among American employees at Marshall and at the other centers, particularly the Johnson Space Flight Center, and at NASA headquarters in Washington. At Marshall, there was resentment about the Germans being the favored group of employees.

> A longtime administrator at Marshall said they complained about [Operation] Paperclip because Germans were being hired instead of Americans. . . . Furthermore, Paperclip recruits received preferential treatment over Americans at Marshall because the top officials were themselves German. (Hunt, 1991, p. 221)

There were other concerns expressed:

> In 1960, a Jewish scientist who had been working with the specialists [von Braun team] for fifteen years revealed his personal impressions in a letter to a close friend. He distinctly remembered the initial shock that an enemy would be imported and placed in a security-conscious atmosphere and, as younger men arrived in large numbers, the discomfort of many Jews in a German atmosphere where English seemed to be a secondary language. . . . He believed that on the surface, at least, the specialists had fit into the "American way of life," and he expressed understanding about their tendency to "gravitate into a clique." But he could not

entirely accept their claim that they were as unaware of the atrocities as the average American was of the true conditions in Sing Sing. "I don't know," he concluded, "I kind of yet see blood on their hands." (Lasby, 1971, p. 215)

This was not the sort of "dirty hands" image the von Braun team had in mind evoking.

Later, as Apollo began to wind down after 1970, the von Braun team began to retire. Some were forced out by the reductions in force that swept NASA during this time. The Germans did not enjoy the veteran's preference, and some retired or left rather than take a reduction in rank leading to a reduced role. Even in the end, the von Braun team felt victimized; they referred to this period at Marshall as the "Great Massacre." Here also, there was probably no intent to hark back to the experience of about a dozen members of the von Braun Team at Mittelbau-Dora, but again, the irony is striking.

Rudolph, a clearly outstanding public manager in the most successful American public organization in modern times and earlier at the Mittelwerk in the Third Reich, retired from NASA with its highest civilian award. He was living quietly in retirement in San Jose, California, collecting his government pension when he was confronted in the early 1980s by the Office of Special Investigations, the Justice Department unit created by Congress in 1979 for the express purpose of pursuing Nazi war criminals living in the United States. Unsurprisingly, surviving members of the von Braun team were an early subject of OSI investigations; some still are (E. Rosenbaum, personal communication, August 4, 1997). In 1984, at the age of 77, Rudolph renounced his U.S. citizenship voluntarily and left the country, after signing an admission that he could not contest the OSI charges in court; in effect, he admitted his guilt. He did not lose his federal pension, however. During the OSI interrogation, Rudolph was shown photographs of the crematorium at Dora, and the following dialogue ensued:

> "Did you ever see it?" asked Sher, referring to the crematorium.
>
> "From the distance, yes."
>
> "And you knew that prisoners who died at Mittelwerk were cremated at the crematorium. You knew that, didn't you?" (Rudolph nodded his head in agreement). "Turn to the next page, Mr. Rudolph. You'll see pictures of prisoners who worked at Mittelwerk when they were liberated by the Allies." The photograph showed a truckload of dead prisoners whose bodies were nothing more than skeletons. "Do those people look like they were working under good conditions?"
>
> "No, certainly not."
>
> "You know the figures are that nearly twenty thousand people died during your service at this facility?"
>
> "No."
>
> "Twenty thousand. Did that . . . would that surprise you?"
>
> "To me, yes."
>
> "You knew people were dying?"
>
> "Oh, yeah. I knew that." (Hunt, 1991, p. 243)

Wernher von Braun died in 1977, so he never had to suffer the final indignity of a war crimes investigation by OSI. In 1985, a 40th anniversary reunion and celebration of the von Braun team's arrival in the United States was held in Huntsville. Rudolph was invited back, and attempts were made to obtain a temporary visa for him. These efforts failed. Rudolph died on January 1, 1996, in Hamburg, Germany, at the age of 89.

Administrative Evil

As discussed in the preceding chapter, during the Holocaust administrative evil went unmasked for all to see, and certainly evil went unmasked at Mittelbau-Dora, where Rudolph completed the first leg of his highly successful career as a manager. It was American public policy and our own public servants, however, who placed the mask on this administrative evil, under Operations Overcast and Paper-clip, and brought it to the United States in the form of some of the members of the von Braun team. That history now tarnishes what many Americans regard as our nation's single greatest technological achievement. Colonel Toftoy and the other technicians representing Army Ordnance may or may not have been truly aware of the evil that was Dora, but what is clear is that their single-minded pursuit of their narrow technical goal blinded them to larger issues that mattered a great deal, at a minimum to Dora's survivors. Or perhaps they simply failed to notice at all. In the modern age, it is the height of irony that in the narrow pursuit of technical superiority, they in essence made a Faustian bargain with administrative evil; we now find that evil sullying our nation's single greatest technical achievement, the moon landing.

5

Organizational Dynamics
and Administrative Evil

The Marshall Space Flight Center, NASA,
and the Space Shuttle Challenger

Societal rules for interaction combine with rules specific
to the organization (standard operating procedures, formal rules, the organization chart, resource allocation), creating a bias for "what has come before." This is meant,
not to deny the decision maker's experience of free will
and rational choice when making a decision, but to point
to the subtle prerational dynamic by which institutional
and organizational arrangements determine the range
of choices that people will see as rational in a given
situation.

—*Diane Vaughan (1996, p. 197)*

◆ In this chapter, we examine the role of the Marshall
Space Flight Center in the space shuttle *Challenger*
disaster with a focus on how less visible dynamics of organizational culture can lead to administrative evil. The *Challenger* disaster was not a case of anyone intending to engage
in evil activity. In fact, in those particular instances in which

actions that some might label as evil took place, new analyses have cast doubt on those interpretations (Vaughan, 1996). Thus, we view the case of Marshall, NASA, and the *Challenger* not as a simple and clear-cut case of administrative evil, but as an opaque and complex—and therefore typical—case in which administrative evil is not only difficult to see but also has a presence that is subject to varying interpretations and conclusions. Such opacity and complexity are hallmarks of administrative evil in our own time and in our own culture.

We are able to identify destructive organizational dynamics within the Marshall Space Flight Center and to some degree in NASA more generally. We believe these dynamics represent a typical organizational pathway that can lead to administrative evil *when no one intends evil*. The absence of evil intentions is another hallmark of administrative evil as it manifests in organizations. A defensive organizational culture at the Marshall Space Flight Center, which was quite functional under the leadership of Wernher von Braun, became destructive as the environment surrounding it became less favorable and as its leadership turned in an arrogant-vindictive direction.

When dealing with inherently risky technology, like an experimental aircraft or a space shuttle, both test pilots and astronauts understand that, say, one in a hundred flights represents the probability of an accident with loss of life—a "normal" accident, if you will. In the space shuttle program, the organizational dynamics at Marshall and, to a lesser extent, within NASA as an organization led to a much greater degree of risk, such that even if the *Challenger* launch had been stopped, the likelihood of a shuttle disaster was far higher than it should have been and a disaster would have likely happened anyway—most likely sooner rather than later. Marshall and NASA's environment, especially the political and budgetary climate, made those decisions that escalated risks substantially appear to be good ones, particularly from the perspective of technical rationality. Even in the absence of evil intentions, organizational dynamics that escalate the chances of disastrous outcomes can be termed administrative evil if the members of an organization could have—and should have—reasonably been expected to do better. We believe that such was the case with the space shuttle program, but even those who may disagree with our interpretation can still see how ordinary—though in most cases less visible—organizational dynamics can create a pathway leading to administrative evil.

The Marshall Space Flight Center, *Challenger*, and the Pathway to Administrative Evil

On January 28, 1986, the space shuttle *Challenger* was launched at 11:38 a.m. Slightly more than a minute later, it exploded, killing all seven people on board. Among the seven on board was Christa McAuliffe, the "teacher in space" who was also the first civilian to participate in a manned space flight. The presidential commission that examined the incident called the event an "accident" (Rogers, 1986). Others refer to it as a disaster, because there was prior knowledge of the O-ring problem (the cause of the explosion) and because two of NASA's contractors actually recommended against launching during the sequence of events leading up to the launch. In other words, this was an event that might have been prevented. Both people and organizations made mistakes in launching *Challenger* that led to a catastrophe and the loss of seven lives (Romzek & Dubnick, 1987). We do not propose to label these "mistakes" as administrative evil.

If an individual had used a gun to kill the seven astronauts or had detonated a hidden bomb on the *Challenger*, we would be more likely to call such action evil. Identifying a single, individual perpetrator helps us name an action as evil. From the victim's perspective—in this case, the surviving victims were the families of the seven astronauts—there might be an inclination, if it was believed that the disaster was preventable, to call at least some of the activities "evil." Still, the presidential commission not only omitted any mention of evil but also termed the catastrophe an "accident," which virtually no one would call evil. Whether some of the actions in this case can be termed as evil is arguable, but the organizational dynamics evident in the case help illustrate how administrative evil can and does emerge within organizations, they help us understand how normal organizational interaction typically masks administrative evil.

A Flawed Design

We know that it was the failure of an O-ring (a rubber seal that is a larger version of the O-ring used in a faucet) that caused the *Challenger* to explode. We also know that the space shuttle, like any complex mechanical system, inherently involves risk. In complex systems, risk is always present and accidents are "normal" (Perrow, 1984). Cars, airplanes, experimental aircraft, and space shuttles have accidents, some of which are catastrophic and lead to loss of life. Some have argued that thinking of such accidents in terms of causation, let alone blame or culpability, may be misguided. They suggest that accidents are simply an inherent result of the risk that is present in all the technological systems that pervade modern society.

This argument has validity in the sense that, in launching some number of space shuttles, a crash is bound to happen at some point. Perfection in technical systems (really, sociotechnical systems) is not possible because of both flaws in materials and human error. Indeed, in the early 1980s, the

Air Force did its own risk assessment of a shuttle crash and calculated a 1 in 35 probability of such a crash. Prompted by that assessment, it removed its satellites from the shuttle's payload roster, reasoning that they could achieve better reliability with ordinary rockets. NASA management, by contrast, assessed the probability of a shuttle crash at an astonishing 1 in 100,000. Such an estimate, it turned out, was symptomatic of some of the problems NASA developed as an organization and that contributed materially to the risk of a disaster. Nobel Prize-winning physicist Richard Feynmann, a member of the Presidential Commission on the Space Shuttle Challenger Accident, conducted his own investigation into NASA's inflated failure estimates. He reached the following conclusions:

> If a reasonable launch schedule is to be maintained, engineering often cannot be done fast enough to keep up with the expectations of originally conservative certification criteria designed to guarantee a very safe vehicle. In these situations, subtly, and often with apparently logical arguments, the criteria are altered so that flights may still be certified in time. They therefore fly in a relatively unsafe condition, with a chance for failure on the order of a percent (it is difficult to be more accurate).
> Official management, on the other hand, claims to believe the probability of failure is a thousand times less. One reason for this may be an attempt to assure the government of NASA perfection and success in order to ensure the supply of funds. The other may be that they sincerely believe it to be true, demonstrating an almost incredible lack of communication between themselves and their working engineers. (Rogers, 1986, p. F-1)

What we see in the case of Marshall and NASA are a series of organizational decisions and reactions that, over time, created a far greater likelihood of disaster than should have been the case (Vaughan, 1996, p. 406).

NASA's History as an Organization

NASA was created in 1958, largely as a response to the sense of emergency that arose from the Soviet Union's launching of the Sputnik I satellite in 1957 (Rosholt, 1966). The image of American technological and military superiority had been fundamentally challenged by our global Cold War competitor. What NASA as an organization subsequently accomplished in 10 short years—landing people on the moon—has few parallels in either the public or private sectors; NASA met the challenge issued by President Kennedy to win the race to the moon. Its early success, however, set the stage for later travails (Schwartz, 1990).

NASA began with about 4,000 employees, doubled by 1960, and reached a peak of 36,000 employees in 1966 (McCurdy, 1993). In the same time period, the NASA budget increased eightfold, peaking at about $5 billion in 1965; this was 0.8% percent of the U.S. gross national product (GNP) for that year. This is stunning growth, and whatever else may be said about NASA, it deserves much credit for successfully achieving its goals in the midst of such growth.

This growth, however, was short-lived, and NASA, like many organizations more recently, experienced real challenges in downsizing (McCurdy, 1993). NASA actually began to contract in 1967, before the Apollo moon landing. The NASA budget shrank each year and fell to 0.2% of the GNP in 1975. NASA employment likewise fell from its peak of 36,000 to 22,000 in 1975. The number of contractor employees funded by NASA shrank from more than 300,000 in 1966 to 100,000 by 1972. Both budget levels and number of employees remained roughly the same through 1990 (although for the budget, this represented a decline in real dollars for nearly a decade, until a couple of spikes in the 1980s). In 1965, NASA's budget of $5.2 billion represented about 5.3% of the entire federal budget. If NASA had had the same share of the 1992 federal budget, its budget would have been $65 billion; its actual 1992 budget was $15 billion.

During NASA's first 10 years, it earned a reputation as a high-performing organization with a "can do" attitude. Since that time, it has settled into a performance level consistent with older, more stable private and public sector organizations. As we shall see, there were several NASA idiosyncrasies that turned out to make matters worse. For one thing, NASA had what might be termed a "mission crisis" after the successful moon shot. What could any organization do for an encore after "one small step for man; one giant leap for mankind"? For another, NASA used a management system fully consonant with the narrow perspective of technical rationality—that is, what NASA called "project management"—and it faltered under the stress of resource stability and decline. NASA also pursued a system of decentralized management for the shuttle program, as opposed to the more centralized system of the Apollo program. This may seem benign on the surface, but a decentralized system renewed and considerably exacerbated competition and division between the three space centers: Johnson, Marshall, and Kennedy. This was particularly significant because it was a key factor, along with leadership changes, in shifting the organizational dynamics of Marshall from defensive but relatively benign under Wernher von Braun to dysfunctional and destructive in the 1970s and 1980s.

Problems in the Apollo Program

It is often forgotten that nearly 20 years before the *Challenger* disaster, there was another conflagration that resulted in the loss of three astronauts' lives. On January 27, 1967— 19 years and 1 day before the *Challenger* disaster—the Apollo I crew died in a prelaunch simulation that resulted in a fatal fire in the command module. This tragedy delayed the Apollo program for 18 months. Some have observed similarities in the two disasters, which would be troubling if it indicated that NASA had not learned from the 1967 incident and simply repeated the same mistakes, but there were important differences as well.

In the Apollo tragedy, there was also a design flaw—the space module operated with a pure oxygen atmosphere, which was highly flammable. All it would take to start a fire was a spark or even static electricity. Compounding this error was that the door to the module did not have an explosive escape device, which meant that it took the ground crew a full 5 minutes to open the hatch door; the astronauts themselves were unable to open the door quickly enough in the midst of a fire. There had been debate in the Apollo program about the best atmosphere for the crew compartment, but most of the discussion focused on the best atmosphere *in flight*, for obvious enough reasons. Not enough thought was devoted to risk factors during simulations on the ground.

As with the shuttle program, there had been reports, both from internal reviews and from whistle-blowers, that raised safety concerns (Brooks, Grimwood, & Swenson, 1979; Phillips, 1965). Both of these suggested that concern for meeting flight schedules (in the case of Apollo, remember, it was a *race* to the moon) negatively affected reliability (safety). There was also concern about cost overruns, but this was different from the cost-cutting at nearly every point in the shuttle program.

Important Differences Between Apollo and the Shuttle

The closest parallel between the Apollo fire and the shuttle explosion was that essentially the same philosophy of management was present within NASA during both time periods—the so-called project management, which sought to balance cost, schedule, and weight while maintaining reliability. In the case of the shuttle, cost considerations were paramount from the very beginning. Conceived first by Wernher von Braun in the 1950s and then advanced by NASA not long after the moon shot, the shuttle itself was a relatively minor appendage to a grander design for a space station. NASA's new dream, conceived by von Braun, was for an elaborate space station in earth orbit, to be serviced by a fleet of space shuttles. Federal budget constraints during the Nixon administration dictated putting the space station on indefinite hold and selling the shuttle as a valuable project in its own right.

The shuttle program was grossly oversold and underbudgeted from the beginning. In 1972, NASA promised 60 shuttle flights per year. In 1983 and 1984, as the shuttle became "operational," there were four and five flights, respectively, with a peak of nine in 1985. Budgetary cost constraints were programwide, but most vivid in retrospect was NASA's choice of Morton Thiokol's design for the solid rocket booster (SRB), used to rocket the shuttle into space. NASA engineers at the Marshall Space Flight Center in the early 1970s referred to Morton Thiokol's design as "unacceptable." NASA management cited Thiokol's "substantial cost advantage" as the chief reason for awarding the contract for the SRB to Morton Thiokol. In 1977 and 1978, NASA engineers at Marshall again raised concerns over this fatal design flaw.

In the case of Apollo, the schedule pressures arose from the competition to be first on the moon. With the shuttle, NASA's scheduling woes were self-inflicted. It sold the shuttle to Congress as a kind of "space truck," with airliner-like reliability (60 flights per year). In part, this was done because the political and budgetary climate effectively demanded it. As Vaughan stated regarding NASA's leadership:

> [It] made decisions and took actions that compromised both
> the shuttle design and the environment of technical deci-
> sion making for work groups throughout the NASA-contrac-
> tor system. Congress and the White House established goals
> and made resource decisions that transformed the R&D
> space agency into a quasi-competitive business operation,
> complete with repeating production cycles, deadlines, and
> cost and efficiency goals. (1996, p. 389)

NASA scaled these early flight estimates back: In 1983, it
promised 24 flights per year by the mid-1980s; in 1986, just
before *Challenger*, it again promised the same 24 flights, but
by 1988. President Reagan had declared the shuttle "fully
operational" (using language provided by NASA) in 1982
after only four flights. This meant that less funding would
be available for any still-needed design work (such as redes-
igning the flawed field joint and its O-rings) and that expectations for the number of flights would escalate.

In the case of Apollo, there had been discussion of the
command module atmosphere. With the shuttle, NASA engineers had flagged an unacceptable design even before the
contract was awarded. When the O-ring design (using a
clevis and tang approach) turned out even worse than
expected in flight, concern mounted. As shuttle flights continued, the O-rings did not "seat" (that is, provide a good
seal) as expected, and compounding the problem, hot gases
from inside the rocket "blew by," eroding not only the primary seal but the secondary seal as well. In 1982, NASA
officially reclassified the SRB joints from "criticality 1R"
(meaning that a failure would be catastrophic, but that it was
a redundant system—by having a second, backup O-ring) to
"criticality 1" (meaning that the backup did not work and
could not be counted on—no redundancy). As the presidential commission noted (Rogers, 1986, p. 148), "The Space
Shuttle's Solid Rocket Booster problem began with the faulty
design of its joint and increased as both NASA and contractor

management (Thiokol) first failed to recognize it as a problem, then failed to fix it, and finally treated it as an acceptable
flight risk."

In August, 1985, a briefing was held at NASA headquarters on the O-ring problem, in which resiliency—the ability
of the O-ring to return to a normal shape from an oval shape
(which was negatively affected by colder temperatures; that
is, the colder the temperature, the longer it took for the seal
to return to its round shape)—was highlighted as the number
one concern. Marshall management insisted on recommend-
ing that flights continue as attempts were made to rectify the
field joint problem. This decision was what NASA headquarters
wanted to hear, but it effectively escalated the risk of disaster
to the point that it was only a matter of time before a disaster
occurred. The decision was conditioned by the destructive
organizational culture that had developed at Marshall.

In the Apollo disaster, there was no contractor recommendation to halt the simulation, nor was there abnormal pressure applied to continue the exercise. Both occurred with
Challenger. The "teacher in space" was a specific White
House initiative from the 1984 campaign and was viewed by
NASA management as a significant strategy to renew public
interest in the shuttle program:

> They established a policy that allowed nonastronauts on
> shuttle missions. Neither official investigation pursued the
> question of who actually decided that a teacher should fly
> on the Challenger mission. By limiting their agenda to the
> technical failure and decision making about the technology,
> the investigations effectively prevented the NASA-White
> House negotiations that culminated in the Teacher in Space
> mission from becoming a matter of public concern.
> (Vaughan, 1996, p. 390)

The president's state of the union address was scheduled for
the evening of January 28, and he was expected to report on

his conversation with Christa McAuliffe in space. The flight had already been delayed from January 26.

The *Challenger* Disaster

A wild card was introduced into the equation when it became apparent that record low temperatures were expected the night before the launch. The coldest prior launch (January, 1985) had been at a seal temperature of 53 degrees; this launch looked like it would take off at below-freezing temperatures. Because cold temperatures, which seriously affected resiliency, had been flagged as the number one concern on O-ring erosion, this news could not have been more unwelcome at Morton Thiokol, where engineers rather quickly agreed that this launch should be stopped if the expected low temperatures materialized.

A teleconference on the evening before the launch was convened between Thiokol, the Marshall Space Flight Center, and the Kennedy Space Center to present the Thiokol engineers' concerns. They recommended against launching at a temperature below 53 degrees. To put this recommendation in context, throughout NASA's history the practice had always been that a contractor's role was to show NASA that its system was safe and ready to launch. That is, the contractor had an affirmative responsibility to show NASA it was safe to "go." In this particular instance, something completely different happened. NASA managers, affiliated with the Marshall Space Flight Center, now put Thiokol management in the position of proving that it was *unsafe* to launch—a complete reversal of standard NASA practice. Thiokol managers got the picture that they were not telling NASA what it wanted to hear, namely, that it was OK to launch. After a recess, Thiokol management, in disregard of their engineers' best thinking, then used the same data charts to "conclude" that launching was OK.

The next day, when it was discovered that there was a significant ice accumulation on the launch pad, Rocco Petrone (who, incidentally, had managed the Apollo program for NASA) of Rockwell International (the prime contractor on the shuttle vehicle itself) directed his representative at the Kennedy Space Center to inform NASA that "Rockwell cannot assure that it is safe to fly" (Meier, 1992, p. 49). This was the second contractor to recommend against launching. In this case, Arne Aldrich of the Johnson Space Flight Center, who was the NASA manager in charge of the shuttle program, suggested that because Rockwell had not insisted against launching, the launch should proceed. The presidential commission noted (Rogers, 1986) that "NASA appeared to be requiring Rockwell to prove that it was not safe to launch rather than proving it was safe" (p. 148). Once again, this was in complete reversal of standard NASA prelaunch practice for its entire history. NASA had never had a contractor recommend against a launch. Not only did NASA find a way to ignore one contractor's initial recommendation not to launch; it ignored two contractors' recommendations against launching.

An Extraordinary Launch

The *Challenger* launch of January 28, 1986, was truly extraordinary, given that NASA had never had a contractor recommend against a launch before and given the reversal of its standard practice of asking contractors to demonstrate that it was safe to launch (Committee on Science and Technology, 1986; Trento, 1987). Three reasons have been advanced for the extraordinary pressure to launch *Challenger* on January 28:

1. The scientific satellite Ulysses, scheduled to be launched on *Challenger*'s next mission, faced a 13-month delay (because of planetary positioning) if flight 51-L did not launch by January 29, the next day.
2. It was generally known, both by NASA and contractors, that President Reagan intended to comment, in his nationally televised state of the union address on the night of January 28, on the liftoff of the first private citizen in space, teacher Christa McAuliffe, and report on his conversation with her in space.
3. The previous shuttle launch, of the *Columbia* on January 12, had earned the record as the most delayed liftoff ever, after seven nonstarts. In addition, flight 51-L's postponements had already received extensive press coverage. (Cook, 1986, p. 20)

In fact, the Ulysses launch actually had a 2-week window beyond January 29, so that issue was not as pressing as it might have been. The latter two reasons surely had some impact, but something beyond these was at work. Richard Cook was one of the two chief whistle-blowers during the *Challenger* investigation and subsequently devoted considerable time to his own investigation of the incident. He made the following statement after speaking with a former Reagan aide in March, 1991:

> I have been told by one eyewitness source that the decision was made by the President of the United States to proceed with the launch in the face of what the President was told were cold weather concerns, because they wanted to get the Shuttle in the air in connection with the publicity for the Teacher-in-Space program. That is where the impetus came from. (Meier, 1992, p. 50)

That phone call (if indeed it was made) would have been made to William Graham, then acting administrator of NASA, who had just recently been brought into the organization as James Beggs's deputy. Beggs fought the appointment of Graham, whose role essentially was to manage the shuttle's planned involvement with the "Star Wars" program, because Graham had no space program experience. Graham subsequently was appointed as the president's science adviser. As acting NASA administrator, Graham would not have been in the normal decision loop for a launch, and it seems reasonable that he may not have known about Thiokol or Rockwell's recommendations not to launch. He certainly was well aware that the "teacher in space" was an important public relations initiative for NASA and that delays in the shuttle's flight schedule were exacting a heavy toll on the agency. Above all, he would have been likely to be quite responsive to a phone call from the president himself.

If indeed President Reagan himself made a phone call to NASA ordering a *Challenger* launch, with the knowledge that there were cold-weather concerns, would it be too great a stretch to call that action evil? Perhaps. We are unlikely to ever know with certainty if the president made such a telephone call, or just how much he knew about or understood the potential risk. If William Graham received such a phone call from the president or even a presidential aide, and subsequently ordered his subordinates to go forward with the launch, would that action be fairly called evil? Perhaps. It becomes more difficult to label as evil the actions of those further down the organizational hierarchy. Many of them were simply being obedient to duly constituted authority, much like the subjects in the Milgram experiments discussed in Chapter 1. It is precisely this sort of ordinary behavior within the Marshall Space Flight Center on which we want to focus more closely, because it is just such ordinary organizational dynamics that enable administrative evil to surface. Indeed, even if the *Challenger* launch had been stopped on that cold January day in 1986, the destructive organizational culture of Marshall had practically ensured a shuttle disaster—it was just a matter of time.

The Marshall Space Flight Center

Morton Thiokol, as the prime contractor on the solid rocket booster, and Marshall, as the project manager for the SRB, were the responsible parties for the field joints and their O-rings, which were a growing problem as shuttle flights continued. The fact that the O-rings were slow to seal was not the predominant problem; rather, it was the hot gas "blow by" that was eroding the O-ring. Once the seal took effect, hot gas no longer got through, but because the O-rings did not seat as quickly as their designers had predicted, there was a longer period of time for the hot gas to escape. This resulted in a potentially deadly race against time during each launch. Hot gas erosion was evident on the second shuttle mission in 1982 but then disappeared for the next seven missions. On the 10th shuttle mission, in 1984, it reappeared. On the subsequent missions (11 through 24), erosion occurred on all but three. The damage was particularly dramatic on mission 15, in January, 1985, during the coldest launch to date—at 53 degrees seal temperature. On that flight, hot gas blow by and erosion had occurred through nearly one third of the circumference of the primary seal but was stopped when the secondary seal functioned properly. On mission 17, the primary seal in a nozzle joint was completely destroyed, and the secondary seal was damaged. If that had occurred in an SRB field joint, that mission would have been lost.

At this time, in mid-1985, Larry Mulloy, the SRB project manager at Marshall, placed a "launch constraint" on the SRB field joints; however, he then subsequently waived the constraint for all of the missions to follow, including that of *Challenger*. A pattern of censoring problematic or negative information for higher-ups within NASA had become evident on Mulloy's part and on Marshall's part more generally. This pattern at Marshall was noted as well on the Hubble

Space Telescope Program, which also had its Program Office at Marshall (Smith, 1989, p. 302). As the Presidential Commission on the Space Shuttle Challenger Accident noted (Rogers, 1986), "neither the launch constraint, the reason for it, or the six consecutive waivers prior to 51-L (Challenger) were known to Moore (Level I) or Aldrich (Level II) or Thomas (the Launch Director at Kennedy)" (p. 84).

A NASA headquarters briefing was held on August 19, 1985 (5 months before *Challenger*), at which O-rings were presented as the chief concern in shuttle safety, and resiliency (that is, the reduced seating capacity of the O-rings as temperatures got colder) as the chief O-ring problem. Marshall staff, however, deleted the following statement from the conclusions chart: "Data obtained on resiliency of the O-rings indicate that lower temperatures aggravate this problem" (Meier, 1992, p. 18). More seriously, they concluded, "It is safe to continue flying" (Meier, 1992, p. 18). Jesse Moore, the NASA Associate Administrator for Space Flight, was briefed on this meeting by his deputy. He followed up by phoning George Hardy, the Deputy Director of Science and Engineering at Marshall, to confirm that the fleet did not need to be grounded until this problem was fixed. Hardy indicated it was safe to fly. This decision was just the latest in a series of decisions made within NASA, Marshall, and Thiokol that, as they accumulated, communicated an acceptance of the safety of the O-rings. This cumulation led to a false sense of security. Larry Mulloy, the SRB project manager, notes that more time and concern were spent on the parachutes that were not functioning properly in returning the spent boosters safely back to the ocean surface so they could be picked up and reused (Vaughan, 1996). The parachutes were so prominent a concern because they had immediate and considerable *cost* implications. Put another way, cost considerations eroded over time the necessary level of attention to safety issues.

The presidential commission included the following among its findings:

1. The commission concluded that there was a serious flaw in the decision-making process leading up to the launch of flight 51-L. A well-structured and managed system emphasizing safety would have flagged the rising doubts about the SRB joint seal. Had these matters been clearly stated and emphasized in the flight readiness process in terms reflecting the views of most of the Thiokol engineers and at least some of the Marshall engineers, it seems likely that the launch of 51-L might not have occurred when it did.

2. The commission was troubled by what appeared to be a propensity of management at Marshall to contain potentially serious problems and to attempt to resolve them internally rather than communicate them forward. The commission saw this tendency as at odds with the need for Marshall to function as part of a system working toward successful flight missions, interfacing and communicating with the other parts of the system that work to the same end. (Rogers, 1986, p. 104)

This tendency within Marshall was fostered by its director, Dr. William Lucas, a veteran of the Apollo program who had been Marshall's director since 1974, following von Braun and the 3-year tenure of Eberhard Rees, a former von Braun deputy and the last of the top Germans. In the 1970s and 1980s, Marshall was run like a Teutonic empire (ironically, this was after nearly all the Germans were gone), with Lucas as its dictator:

This autocratic leadership style grew over the years to create an atmosphere of rigid, often fearful conformity among Marshall managers. Unlike other senior NASA officials, who reprimanded subordinates in private, Lucas reportedly used open meetings to scornfully criticize lax performance. And like many demanding task masters, he demanded absolute personal loyalty. (McConnell, 1987, p. 108)

Essentially, the three centers, Marshall, Johnson, and Kennedy, but particularly the former two, were engaged in a competitive rivalry, and the least favored center would be the one that slowed the launch schedule. Lucas was determined that Marshall would win that competition:

> Lucas' management style, combined with the production pressure the center was experiencing, not only exacerbated the intercenter rivalry but resulted in competition between the three Marshall projects. Each Project Manager vied with the others to conform to the cultural imperatives of the original technical culture. . . . They competed to meet deadlines, be on top of every technical detail, solve their technical problems, conform to rules and requirements, be cost-efficient, and, of course, contribute to safe, successful space-flight. . . . No Project Manager wanted his hardware or people to be responsible for a technical failure. To describe the pressure at Marshall simply as production pressure is to underestimate it. It was, in fact, performance pressure . . . that permeated the workplace culture. (Vaughan, 1996, p. 218)

Lucas let it be known that, under no circumstances, would Marshall be responsible for delaying a launch (McConnell, 1987, p. 109). Indeed, in the 25 Flight Readiness Reviews in the shuttle program's history, not once had Marshall indicated that a launch should not go forward as planned, although it was responsible for a number of the technical glitches that delayed launches.

The Evolution of a Destructive Organizational Culture at Marshall

Wernher von Braun's subordinates, by all accounts, ranked him very high as a manager and leader (Bilstein, 1980). Among members of the von Braun team, this is per-

haps not surprising, because it was his leadership that res-
cued the group from the dead end of postwar Germany,
brought them to a new land, and led them forward to great
accomplishments. His leadership inspired a *Festschrift*,
originally including 40 papers written primarily by his subordinates, in honor of his 50th birthday in 1962. Von Braun
was known to practice his "dirty hands" approach to management by dropping in on one of his prized laboratories and
asking about a detail of which most agency directors would
simply be unaware. His knowledge of technical detail was
legendary, and he successfully negotiated the boundary
between Marshall and NASA headquarters, and more generally, society at large. From his mid-20s until his retirement
in 1972, von Braun held increasingly responsible management positions and exercised clear leadership in all of them.

Von Braun's leadership style was expansive, as manifested in an attempt (Allcorn & Diamond, 1997, p. 27), "to
master and control events and people in order to allay
anxiety." He exhibited clear tendencies toward a "narcissistic" approach to management:

> Projects an image of self-confidence and demands admira-
> tion and loyalty from others. Dreamer and risk taker. . . .
> Develops big ideas and plans which are accompanied by
> boundless energy. (Allcorn & Diamond, 1997, p. 31)

Von Braun's "dirty hands" approach, although quite functional in the context of developing the Saturn and other
rockets, was also a very controlling approach. Von Braun
showed his narcissistic bent in a number of other ways. He
accepted large numbers of public speaking engagements
during the 1950s and 1960s; during the latter decade, the
number of engagements was in apparent violation of NASA
regulations. James Webb, the NASA administrator at the
time, is said to have told von Braun to limit these engage-

ments (McConnell, 1986). Von Braun, during the 1950s, developed a relationship with Walt Disney and even served as a consultant on three Disney space-related films from those years. He clearly saw himself as a visionary for space and its exploration, and he acted in ways that asked—or demanded—that others view him that way. When narcissistic tendencies are carried too far, it becomes easy to denigrate subordinates, as von Braun does subtly in the beginning of a paper written in 1962:

> It is a rare opportunity for me to have an audience of such experienced and distinguished managers. I appreciate the privilege of telling you the same thing everybody else does; namely, that no matter *how* you are running your organization, you are doing it *all* wrong and you should do it *our* way. . . . It takes a manager with a rare sort of ability to get much work out of people and still keep them happy, or at least keep them from fighting in the halls. . . . It is the same rare manager who can pass out the money, assign functions, allot office space, authorize carpets and reorganize the entire outfit without anyone losing face, quitting, or getting drunk on the job. It also takes real managerial talent to pacify employees who often are harassed by headquarters, sometimes outwitted by industry. . . . But it is the greatest manager of all who can keep reasonable peace in the family after he has split all the annual resources among all the department heads. (von Braun, 1963, p. 248)

This beginning was surely written—and probably delivered—with humorous intent by von Braun, yet it reveals his narcissistic bent as a leader.

Although there were problems during von Braun's tenure, Marshall was clearly not only a functional organization but also arguably a high-performing one through the 1960s (McCurdy, 1993). Still, as discussed in Chapter 4, Marshall developed a siege mentality during those years, with the von Braun team always feeling slighted and at times even attacked. At the same time, there were divisions and occasional conflict between the Germans and subordinate Americans at Marshall, as well as with their American superiors at NASA headquarters in Washington. Why did these factors not lead to a destructive culture during von Braun's tenure at Marshall?

Apart from von Braun's and other team members' talents as managers and leaders, which may well have been considerable, one factor in Marshall's (and NASA's) success was a clear sense of mission—this was a *race* to the moon. The resources also were there; this was largely a period of very rapid expansion, which as we have noted represents a serious managerial challenge in itself (a good problem, if you will, but a problem nevertheless). In addition, the "everything under one roof" approach in which Marshall sought to maintain the necessary technical expertise to design and construct in-house, was far stronger in the 1960s than in the 1970s and 1980s. When a defensive organizational culture exists, however, change in the surrounding environment or change in the organization—particularly in leadership—can trigger this potential into destructive dynamics. This appears to have occurred at Marshall.

NASA began to contract as an organization even before the moon landing in 1969. Recall that the budget began to shrink in 1967, and personnel shortly before in 1966. This trajectory increased dramatically as it became clear that the Apollo program was going to wind down in the early 1970s. Remember that this was a period of time that the von Braun team referred to as the "Great Massacre." Marshall's technical culture gradually became more illusion than reality. Also recall that NASA underwent a "mission crisis" at this time. Although Marshall had many projects under way during the 1970s, these were all pale shadows of Apollo. No one was in a race anymore, and NASA was no longer favored with large budgets. As Vaughan (1996) notes, NASA top management made decisions that were significant compromises for the agency:

> They made bargains that altered the organization's goals, structure and culture. These changes had enormous repercussions. They altered the consciousness and actions of technical decision makers, ultimately affecting the Challenger launch deliberations. Also, NASA top administrators responded to an environment of scarcity by promulgating the myth of routine, operational space flight. (p. 390)

This was the context in which Dr. William Lucas assumed leadership at Marshall in 1974. Lucas had spent his entire career at Marshall (and earlier at Redstone)—nearly 25 years at that time. In 1960, the Marshall organizational chart showed Lucas in charge of the Engineering Materials Branch, within the Structures and Mechanics Division under the direction of William Mrazek, one of the von Braun team (Bilstein, 1980, p. 446). As Marshall director, Lucas had those expansive shoes of von Braun's to fill, and also, by comparison, a much less propitious situation in terms of projects, personnel, and budget. There is no way of knowing whether Lucas may have thought he was emulating von Braun's management style, but we do know that his own became quickly apparent:

> Many observers saw Lucas' leadership style as the exact opposite of von Braun. Where von Braun had been a charismatic visionary who instilled loyalty through personal magnetism, Lucas was a coldly distant (and often rigid) master bureaucrat. He believed in doing things by the regulations. Interpreting the regulations was his prerogative. (McConnell, 1986, p. 107)

Vaughan (1996) sheds further light on Lucas's management style:

Saddled with a vastly more complex Marshall organizational structure and apparently lacking von Braun's cha-
risma and skill at maintaining personal contact with people
at different levels in the Marshall hierarchy, Lucas relied on
hierarchy and formal mechanisms to transfer information.
He insisted on bureaucratic accountability for monitoring
and controlling internal operations. (p. 218)

As it happens, this leadership style is closer to von Braun's
than one might at first imagine. He shared with von Braun
an expansive approach; however, in Lucas's case, rather than
a narcissistic style, he manifested an arrogant-vindictive
style (Allcorn & Diamond, 1996, p. 30): "Highly competitive
and must win all encounters at any cost. Intent upon defeat-
ing and humiliating others who harm arrogant pride. Para-
lyzes others with fear by being intimidating."

Under the arrogant-vindictive leadership of William
Lucas and no longer in the exalted (but also defensive)
position as the world's premier rocket facility, Marshall
developed a persecutory organizational identity. The concept of "organizational identity" is defined (Diamond, 1988,
p. 169) as "the totality of repetitive patterns of individual
behavior and interpersonal relationships that taken together
comprise the unacknowledged meaning of organizational
life." These patterns include both conscious and unconscious interaction. They are an important constituent of an
organization's identity and represent a fruitful avenue into
the implicit dimension of organization culture, particularly
at the level of interpersonal and group relations (Adams,
1993; Diamond, 1993). At Marshall, the defensiveness characteristic of the von Braun years escalated under Lucas into
a persecutory organizational identity in which

workers feel powerless and disrespected. They experience
their conflict with the organization and its leadership in a

manner that is passive. . . . Things (decisions and actions) are done to them. They have little say and often feel they have little recourse. . . . The lack of mutual respect between the leadership and the workforce is signified by unilateral . . . top-down executive . . . decisions and actions of an oppressive organizational culture. (Allcorn & Diamond, 1997, pp. 241-242)

Lucas was notorious for reprimanding—or, more accurately, verbally tearing apart—subordinates who made mistakes, in public meetings (R. Boisjoly, personal communication, July 17, 1997). This meant that the preferred choice for Marshall employees was not to make mistakes. With perfection being difficult to produce at all times, camouflaging any mistakes would be the next best bet. Lucas and other managers were quite predictably told what they wanted to hear (no mistakes, no delays, no problems), not what they needed to know (Smith, 1989). Although there were several levels of Flight Readiness Review within Marshall, the highest level, the Marshall Center Board, was notorious:

> The Marshall Center Board FRR was the quintessential embodiment of Marshall culture. Although Marshall's Level IV and III FRRs were adversarial and rigorous, they paled in comparison to the Lucas-embellished culture of the more formal, large-audience Center Board review. The Center Board was the final in-house review before Marshall Level III Project Managers made their assessments of flight readiness at Level II and Level I before Johnson and NASA top administrators respectively. Lucas presided. Here we see the distinctive Marshall performance pressure. (Vaughan, 1996, p. 219)

Vaughan quotes more extensively from a personal interview with Larry Wear, one of Marshall's program managers:

> The Center Board would be held in a humongous conference room that looks like an auditorium. It's an open meeting. There might be one hundred–one hundred fifty people there. . . . It's great drama. . . . and it's an adversarial process. I think there are some people who have, what's the word, there is a word for when you enjoy somebody else's punishment . . . masochistic, they are masochistic. You know, come in and watch Larry Wear or Larry Mulloy or Thiokol take a whipping from the Board. (1996, pp. 219-220)

The decentralization of the space shuttle program office to the Johnson Space Flight Center in Houston (the Apollo Program Office had been at NASA headquarters in Washington) had the added effect of escalating the competition and conflict between the centers that had existed during the von Braun years. This led to Lucas's disastrous insistence that Marshall not be responsible for any launch delays on the shuttle flight program. As Vaughan observes:

> Marshall's concerns about looking good among other centers translated into competition between the SRB, Main Engine, and External Tank Projects at the Center Board FRR. Impression management was the name of the game. Performance pressure resulted in managing impressions by *leaving no stone unturned*. This thoroughness created intense preoccupation with procedural conformity and "going by the book." (1996, p. 220)

Quite apart from the *Challenger* disaster, Marshall's unwillingness to "fail" or "lose" by grounding the fleet until the fatal design flaw could be fixed, and its increasingly rigid and pressurized approach to the Flight Readiness Review process, essentially guaranteed that a shuttle disaster would occur sometime soon.

The Pathway to Administrative Evil

Should we infer from this discussion that NASA as an organization was evil? Or should we conclude that the von Braun team was somehow responsible for the *Challenger* disaster? Of course not—neither would be reasonable conclusions. We can isolate some specific instances in the *Challenger* tragedy that *may* have constituted administrative evil, specifically, if President Reagan indeed made the phone call ordering a launch with full knowledge of the concerns, and if Graham received such a call and passed along the order to launch. The senior management team at Morton Thiokol, in ignoring the best advice of their engineers and caving in to pressure from NASA, a major customer, was at a minimum unethical.

William Lucas's leadership placed Marshall at continuous risk of administrative evil because, even if *Challenger* had not been launched, the destructive patterns of interaction emanating from the persecutory organizational culture virtually ensured a shuttle disaster resulting in the loss of astronauts' lives in the near term. Nobody at the Marshall Space Flight Center, Lucas surely included, set out to do evil, but the destructive organizational culture that manifested itself during and before *Challenger* put lives at unnecessary risk. It would be unfair and unwarranted to connect *Challenger* with the unmasked and essentially transparent administrative evil demonstrated at Mittelbau-Dora and Peenemünde. Operations Overcast and Paperclip, policies of the U.S. government, each abetting administrative evil, represent only an ironic connection to later events at the Marshall Space Flight Center and with *Challenger*. Whatever administrative evil can be legitimately attributed to Marshall is of the typical organizational variety in our time and in our culture. It is opaque and complex, and no one can be identified with evil intentions. It is well masked.

6

Public Policy and
Administrative Evil

Racism is a policy first, ideology second. Like all politics,
it needs organization, managers and experts.
Zygmunt Bauman (1989, p. 74)

◆ In the preceding chapters, we examined how the Holocaust and other, better-masked instances of administrative evil, which have exemplified the technical-rational
approach to administration, encourage public administrators and citizens alike to equate or replace substantive
values with procedural ones. Doing things the right way and
protecting organizational interests can define or supersede
doing the right things and make it easier to commit or
contribute to destructive acts by separating—mentally—the
doer from the deed (Keeley, 1983). Although certainly not
inherently evil, the values of procedural correctness and
efficiency contribute to a blindness to the context in which
they are applied and to the human consequences of administrative action. The purpose of this chapter is to explore the
contemporary context in which public policy is made and
implemented, with a focus on how the tacit assumptions that
undergird technical-rational solutions to messy, intractable

social problems can unwittingly contribute to the break-down of community, the creation of "surplus populations," and, through moral inversions, even to public policies of destruction.

Public Policy and Problem Solving

The modern approach to public policy and planning is summarized best, and most commonly, in terms of the process of problem solving. That is, the purpose of public policy is to identify, develop, and implement solutions to an array of discrete social problems (Schon, 1993). Doing so requires a confluence of scientific method or technology (means) and political will or consensus (ends). This image of public policy as problem solving is realized only in those rather uncommon instances when the technology for addressing the problem is known and a political consensus exists on the goals of the policy. In such rare contexts, public adminis-trators can rationally predict outcomes, focus on optimizing the efficiency and effectiveness of their processes and programs, and be held accountable for their performance (Christensen, 1985). In effect, they can solve policy problems by following scientifically or rationally established proce-dures. In most social policy arenas, this image of public policy as problem solving is largely a fiction.

Public policy as problem solving has its roots in the modern, scientific worldview that seeks to bend nature and society to the will of scientific method and technology (Bauman, 1989; Keller, 1985). As a conceptual framework for thinking about public policy, problem solving implies—and creates the expectation—that a satisfactory end point, a solution, or ideally, elimination of a social problem can be achieved through the application of modern, scientific methods. We are reminded of the common question: Why is it that we can we put a man on the moon but can't find a solution to homelessness (or some other intractable social problem)?

Sending astronauts to the moon was far from the discrete, programmable project with a clear endpoint or goal that our popular understanding implies. As we have seen, it was connected to a public policy—and its implementation—that represented administrative evil, at least in part. The image of engineering and scientific methods as able to assume predictable and stable cause and effect relationships nevertheless endures. The image of the moon project was that specific problems could be identified and addressed according to known procedures by a dedicated workforce. Further, the program was undertaken in a context of considerable political and social consensus—perhaps an all-too-facile consensus. Thus, our social fantasy was that this was a project that could be programmed, implemented, and completed more or less according to plan (Christensen, 1985).

In contrast, racism, discrimination, poverty, crime, drug abuse, illegal immigration, and other social issues transparently do not fit this image of discrete problems that can be solved once and for all with analytic methods. They are complex, lived situations in which cause and effect relations, when they exist at all, are chaotic, shifting, and unpredictable. It is both puzzling and ironic that the technical-rational, problem-solving approach to public policy appears to have more than the cat's nine lives, even as the most recent "solution" is disparaged as too narrow, or insufficiently understood, or as the new problem to be solved. The problem-solving approach has been continually frustrated by the vagaries of human behavior and societal dynamics, yet it perdures. Programmed solutions to such "problems" are partial, temporary, and largely ineffective, and political consensus often is elusive (Blanco, 1994). Furthermore, these solutions often produce unintended consequences (Schon,

1993, p. 144) that "come to be perceived as problems in their own right (as public housing, conceived initially as a solution to the problem of housing the temporarily poor, came later to be perceived as a concentration of social pathology)." As tempting as it has been to use the moon shot or other technological achievements as putative models for solving public policy problems, social problems continue to resist attempts to solve them with specific, rational programs.

Critiques of the Problem-Solving Approach to Public Policy

In recent years, a number of authors (Bauman, 1989; Blanco, 1994; Saul, 1992; Schon, 1993; Stone, 1988; Yanow, 1995) have questioned whether problem solving itself is an appropriate conceptual framework for public policy, especially in the realm of social policy. More than 30 years ago, essentially the same arguments were made by Sir Geoffrey Vickers in *The Art of Judgment* (1965/1995). In the view of these writers, problem solving is a metaphorical, not a literal, way of thinking about governmental responses to undesirable social and economic circumstances. More specifically, it is the basis for generating specific metaphors for understanding social problems. What they see as especially problematic is the extent to which problem solving has attained an unquestioned dominance in the policy arena, with little or no reflection on the possible consequences of addressing social issues in this way. "In order to dissolve the obviousness of diagnosis and prescription in the field of social policy, we need to become aware of, and to focus attention upon, the generative metaphors which underlie our problem-setting stories. Often we are unaware of the metaphors that shape our perception and understanding of social situations" (Schon, 1993, p. 148).

Saul (1992) argues that Western civilization appears unable to deal with its social problems, largely because the "dictatorship of reason" (i.e., technical rationality) has left its leaders with little memory of their history and the social processes and institutions that contributed to contemporary problems. The most common response therefore is to redouble the efforts to solve problems that stem from the uncritical application of technical-rational methods, while overlooking or denying more fundamental issues such as the persistent inability to deal with the problem of racism that underlies the debate over affirmative action, drug policies, and other social policies.

Authors such as Saul (1992), Schon (1993), and Bauman (1989) argue that Western society has placed all its faith and energies at the service of a "single, all purpose elite using a single all-purpose methodology" (Saul, 1992, p. 135). Or, as Bauman (1989, p. 12) puts it, society has put faith in "the chorus of experts who assure us that human problems are matters of wrong policies, and the right policies mean elimination of problems." These technical-rational experts and their scientific methodology work to systematically reduce the fundamental contradictions and ambiguities that characterize social life into formulas and programs. This preintegrated logic, systematically taught at the leading institutions of higher learning as policy analysis, seeks to drive out contradiction and pursues efficient solutions to messy social problems.

These critiques strike at the heart of modern public administration and policy making. As we saw in Chapter 2, much of modern public administration can be seen as the logical heir of the Enlightenment and the critical power of rational methods that were so skillfully wielded by Voltaire and his contemporaries against the oppression of the *ancien régime* and the superstitions of medieval society. Saul

(1992), for example, maintains that the liberating powers of reason ultimately were harnessed not by the champions of common sense and democracy (e.g., Voltaire and Jefferson) but by the courtesans and dictators, or technocrats and experts, who use reason in pursuit of power and unrestrained personal ambition. Thus, the progenitors of contemporary Western civilization are Machiavelli, Ignatius Loyola, Cardinal Richelieu, and Napoleon. Their legacy can be found in a society dominated by skilled technicians and administrators who employ sophisticated techniques in the service of complex, self-referential systems that bear an eerie resemblance to the autocratic medieval institutions undermined by the Enlightenment and that are all too capable of complicity in administrative evil.

Saul (1992) offers Robert McNamara as a contemporary paragon of the rule of reason, or, as "the individual who most dramatically fills the role of the man of reason in flamboyant decline" (p. 81). McNamara's career at the apex of the administrative elite in both the public and private sectors was guided by the conviction that the careful application of reason, logic, and efficiency inevitably produces good. For him, technical rationality and morality are inextricably linked. The full development of a technical-rational, professional expertise stems from a moral imperative that, when applied to human and organizational problems, will produce the right answers and effective solutions. In the wake of McNamara's career (and those of others like him) we find nothing short of "uncontrollable disasters from which the West has still not recovered" (Saul, 1992, p. 81).

As Secretary of Defense, McNamara began the process of "professionalizing" the armed forces that led to the creation of a worldwide arms trading system that grew to influence and distort the world economy. When events in the Vietnam War spun out of control, he resigned as Secretary of Defense in the midst of moral outrage against the war he had helped engender. McNamara went from there to head the World Bank, where his policies contributed to a worldwide debt problem that continues to stagger not only Third World economies but those of the West as well. Although he has admitted, after nearly three decades and near the end of his career, that the Vietnam War was a mistake, McNamara apparently has not realized that his approach to public policy problems might be flawed, nor has he considered that reason reduced to rationality drives out moral considerations subtly but decisively, thus paving the way for moral inversion. This is one of the masks that administrative evil wears.

Saul (1992) finds the fundamental flaw of technical-rational management in its lack of historical consciousness or denial of the past, because it is as an uncontrollable element. For the technocrat, past failures cannot have resulted from the application of rational methods; they must be the result of having been insufficiently rational. If events did not turn out as planned, the problem is not with the policy but instead is a result of uncontrolled deviations from it. Hence, we need more and better planning, and more efficient, controlled systems that will preclude messy aberrations. Although the past confronts us with the complexities of a socially constructed reality, the future represents a pristine canvas on which to impose new rational plans and systems, with the present always subject to technical control. The lack of historical consciousness is virtually an open invitation to administrative evil.

The linking of technical rationality and morality not only leads to frustration with failed solutions to social problems; it also can set the stage for administrative evil because rational programming in human affairs inevitably entails some degree of dehumanization and often involves restrictions on the political rights of those affected (Bauman, 1989; Rubenstein, 1975, 1983). To the extent that "good" is expected to result from rational solutions to perceived problems, obstacles to these programs cannot be tolerated. This approach invokes metaphors of removal or elimination, like pulling weeds from a carefully cultivated garden (Bauman, 1989, p. 18) or ridding an organism of a disease (Schon, 1993). In cases of moral inversion, when something evil is repackaged or otherwise redefined as good, great eruptions of administrative evil may occur.

Engineered or programmed solutions to social problems can achieve only limited success in eliminating a problem when programs are constrained by concerns about the political rights and humanity of the target population. For example, the "crime problem" could perhaps be solved if police were allowed to conduct investigations without regard for the civil rights of suspects, as they are in some countries. Illegal drug trafficking could perhaps be reduced to near zero if property could be searched and seized without warrants, and if suspects could be tortured or shot on the spot. Illegal immigration could be greatly reduced by barricading the borders of Texas, New Mexico, Arizona, and California (a reverse Berlin Wall staffed by special forces with orders to shoot to kill) and by incarcerating captured violators in concentration camps, thus discouraging prospective violators by making failure too costly. Public policy appears to be moving in these directions, but not dramatically—only in successive, small increments.

In the United States, many such problems remain unsolved in part because the polity maintains an "uneasy equilibrium" (Berlin, 1991) between competing values rather than an unambiguous pursuit of final, and potentially inhumane, solutions to social problems. The drive to solve social problems has thus been balanced with concern for political and human rights. This equilibrium becomes most tenuous when the problem involves "surplus populations" (Rubenstein, 1975, 1983), that is, defined groups of people who are made to appear "useless," or worse, who are viewed as detrimental to the well-being of everyone else—scapegoats or victims. When the objects of public policy programs are rendered "socially dead" (Goldhagen, 1996) and portrayed as unwanted vermin or disease in the midst of society (Bauman, 1989), the resulting moral inversion may unleash tendencies toward administrative evil and policies of elimination or even extermination.

Surplus Populations and Public Policy Metaphors

It is easy to think of extermination as an extreme measure, but it may not be perceived as such an extreme act when the object of extermination is considered dangerous, out of place, or unwanted, and when it is preceded by a series of successively more aggressive measures, each of which—relatively innocuous by itself—extends the boundary of the acceptable. We routinely exterminate vermin from buildings, spray chemical pesticides on destructive insects or plants that invade our crops, and euthanize animals in pounds and shelters. Such actions are perceived as routine and justifiable (by those doing the exterminating) because the object of extermination is not human and not perceived as belonging to anyone, or alternatively is seen as a threat to the well-being of society. Eliminating the smallpox virus, for example, has been a great benefit to humankind, bringing an end to one of the most lethal and widespread contagions in human history. In such cases, extermination represents an efficient and effective solution to difficult problems.

Successful application of modern scientific methods to eliminate or control agricultural and medical problems has contributed to the introduction of agricultural and medical metaphors into public policy discourse. Eliminating blight, contagion, or cancerous growths in the body politic through the application of expert knowledge and methods has become a common means of understanding how to solve many difficult policy problems (e.g., urban decay, illicit drugs, illegal immigration). The desire to eliminate such problems, and, by extension, the potential surplus populations with which they are associated, often forms the hidden metaphorical subtext of the search for solutions.

Rubenstein (1983, p. 1) defines a surplus population as "one that for any reason can find no viable role in the society in which it is domiciled." He argues that the overproduction of people and concomitant programs for their elimination are central features of modern civilization. A variety of eliminationist programs have been pursued by governments throughout the world during the modern period (e.g., the Irish famine, U.S. policy toward Native Americans, the Armenian genocide, forced collectivization and starvation in the Soviet Union, the Great Leap Forward in China, the Holocaust). These are all, as (Rubenstein, 1987) notes, "alternative attempts to solve a common problem, one of getting rid of people whom governments perceive to be without function or otherwise undesirable" (p. 9). In contrast, many of the social policies of the post-World War II era represented a proactive effort by government to include formerly unwanted or marginal people in the mainstream of American society. The present willingness to abandon such policies without seeking alternative approaches may lead to the creation of new surplus populations in the United States (Rubenstein, 1975): "The history of the twentieth century has taught us that people who are rendered permanently superfluous are eventually condemned to segregated precincts of the living dead or are exterminated outright" (p. 96).

Again, the Holocaust is instructive because it provides the clearest historical link between the search for permanent solutions to problems and eliminationist policy. The policies of separation (definition and concentration) and elimination of the Jews from German and European society were often expressed through metaphors of disease and blight (Bauman, 1989; Glass, 1997; Goldhagen, 1996). The poverty and misery of the Jewish ghettos in Poland intensified and gave meaning to German anti-Semitism and to the association of Jews with vermin. Descriptions of ghettos suggested that the whole of Polish Jewry was one large diseased entity. For example, a government sponsored magazine commented in 1944 about the conditions in German-administered Poland:

> Millions of Jews lived amidst other ethnic groups in the territory of today's Government General. Here, in the breeding ground of modern World Jewry, the Jewish Problem reached its zenith. . . . We had a moral obligation to wipe out the breeding places of the most horrendous, the most inhuman, and the most beastly vice that, arising from Poland, infested the whole world. It was a task which, in its fulfillment, was meant to bring salvation to the whole of humanity. (Dwork & van Pelt, 1996, p. 37)

The metaphors of disease and vermin thus provided the conceptual framework that guided the search for a "final solution" to the "Jewish problem."

Contemporary social problems are often framed in very similar terms. Consider the metaphorical language used to describe urban slums and the problem of urban decay in the United States:

> The experts concluded that if the community were to be healthy, if it were not to be revert again to a blighted or slum area, as though possessed of a congenital disease, the area must be planned as a whole. It was not enough, they believed, to remove existing buildings that were unsanitary or unsightly. It was important to redesign the whole area so

as to eliminate the conditions that cause slums. . . . In this
way it was hoped that the cycle of decay of the area could
be controlled and the birth of future slums prevented.
(Bellush & Hausknecht, 1967, p. 62)

Eliminating the "blighted" conditions that cause slums
entailed the dismantling and displacement of entire communities. Although downtown areas were "renewed," many of
those who were displaced were only shifted to other slums
(Katz, 1989, p. 136), keeping the surplus populations out of
sight and mind of newly gentrified neighborhoods and com-
mercial/entertainment districts. Fortunately, what many
came to call "Negro removal" did not escalate to eliminationist policies.

Other approaches to urban policy are driven out by the
underlying metaphor of blight and disease. Little room for
alternatives to eliminating the slums exists when action is
driven by such tacit concepts that are, at best, poor descrip-
tors of the actual conditions to be addressed by the policy.

> It is precisely because neighborhoods are not literally dis-
> eased that one can *see* them *as* diseased. It is because urban
> communities are not literally natural that one can see them
> as natural. In this "seeing-as" we construct what is wrong
> and what needs fixing. (Schon, 1993, p. 150)

Other dangerous, contemporary metaphors of public policy tend to identify the cause of social disease or decay not
as stemming from race or ethnicity but as residing in individual behaviors and environmental conditions. The job of
the policy expert is conceived of as ridding society of the
behaviors and conditions that are deemed inconsistent with
dominant norms and visions of the good life. Even while
policy makers decry racism rhetorically, the effect of policies
can be to marginalize populations and groups that do not
conform to definitions of normality and social health.

Welfare Policy and
Illegal Drug Policy

Two such problem areas around which a considerable societal consensus has developed are those of welfare dependence and illicit drug use. Both are seen as threats to the very fabric of society and as meriting vigorous efforts to achieve a lasting solution. Long-term welfare recipients are characterized as moral degenerates who avoid or disdain work, and who take advantage of the tax dollars taken from hardworking citizens. The concept of the "underclass" has given expression to the notion that an undeserving and possibly genetically inferior, poor population undermines the moral order of society (e.g., Herrnstein & Murray, 1994; Murray, 1984). "They" have all but become a surplus population.

The proposed "solution" to this problem entails a work requirement and strict time limits on the receipt of benefits. The belief that virtually any work builds character and fulfills social obligations underlies these programs (Katz, 1989). The possibility that the economy may not provide the needed jobs has not been given adequate consideration. The fact that the majority of those affected by the policy are children does not seem to matter, unless it becomes a political issue (Edelman, 1977). Empirical evidence that contradicts the assumptions of reformers has done little to dissuade those who would force welfare recipients to work (Jencks, 1992; Katz, 1989). That welfare dependence is a problem of "their" moral deficiency, to be solved by compulsory work, has become the conventional wisdom.

Poverty thus is no longer a legitimate reason for entitlement to government benefits. In fact, welfare is now the problem to be solved, not poverty. "Welfare queens" and others dependent on welfare will be "freed" from their bondage to the system through the medium of work. Welfare recipients will be required to work for their benefits and can receive those benefits only for a limited time period (arbitrarily set at 2 years in most states). During that time, they will be monitored carefully for proper behavior and, in a growing number of jurisdictions, even fingerprinted to ensure they do not collect extra benefits. Once that period is up, benefits will end. Those who refuse to work will be forced to confront the hard lessons of the marketplace. They must learn to work or face the consequences. In a classic instance of moral inversion, this is called "empowerment" by some.

Looking at this approach to welfare reform through the window of the Holocaust, as Bauman (1989) would suggest, we can see, with chilling effect, similarities between it and Nazi beliefs and policies toward the Jews. The Nazis, consistent with a long heritage of anti-Semitism, portrayed the Jews as parasites "whose working lives were devoted to feeding on the blood of the industrious German people" (Goldhagen, 1996, p. 285). This belief was not to be shaken by contrary evidence. Nor did it matter whether the work was productive or not—the Jew must work. Even as they planned and carried out destruction of the Jews, the Nazis felt it necessary to put them to work, to punish them for their supposed slothfulness and to demonstrate German mastery over the Jewish race. The infamous sign hanging over the entrance to Auschwitz and other concentration camps expressed this moral inversion to perfection: "Arbeit Macht Frei" (work makes freedom).

The point of this discussion is not to say that those who advocate a particular approach to welfare reform are Nazis or have genocidal intent, but to highlight the dangers inherent in an approach that tacitly defines and then dehumanizes a surplus population. To use Schon's (1993) terms, the welfare problem has been framed in a way that relieves society of any responsibility for those who do not succeed under the new policy. Undoubtedly some will succeed, but others will not. What will happen to those who cannot find adequate employment after their benefits run out? Who will ensure that the children are educated and healthy? Is society willing to invest sufficient resources to ensure that everyone who wants to work has a job? What solution will society employ if confronted with growing numbers of surplus people who are deemed unworthy of public support? Rubenstein raises a chilling possibility:

> There could come a time when bureaucrats might attempt to eliminate all of the ills associated with urban blight, such as crime, drugs, and unsafe streets, by eliminating those segments of the population that are regarded as prone to social pathology. The Germans had such a program in mind when they planned to eliminate "asocials" from German society by exterminating them. Is it possible, for example, that some future American administration might solve the problem of non-white "welfare loafers" who are "too lazy to work" by such measures? (1975, pp. 85-86)

To some extent, one answer can be seen in current policies toward the sale and use of illegal drugs. Prisons are overflowing throughout the country, and corrections budgets are swelling in an effort to incarcerate the large numbers of drug users and dealers who are being sentenced to long terms in state and federal prisons. This is occurring despite the tenuous relationship between the legality of drugs and the harm that each may cause (Ostrowski, 1989, cited in Meier, 1994). The "war on drugs" is waged against substances that arguably cause much less harm to society as a whole than legal narcotics such as tobacco and alcohol. As the incarceration "solution" inexorably unfolds to its logical conclusion, governments, under the leadership of those who would "get government off our backs," enthusiastically invest huge sums of public money in the building and maintenance of prisons. This policy reminds us of the propensity of modern governments and societies to define and then concentrate a surplus population (Hirsch, 1995; Horowitz, 1980; Kuper, 1981; Smith, 1987; Staub, 1989). Proposals to expand the death penalty for drug dealers suggest that the limits for how to dispose of this growing surplus population have not yet been reached.

Again, the argument here is not that drugs ought to be legalized, that their abuse is not a problem, or that we are (currently) a genocidal society. The difficulty stems not from the problem itself but from the way in which it is framed or defined (Schon, 1993). It has become almost impossible for politicians to ask whether our current approaches to drug policies are worth pursuing, even as costs mount and drug use continues unabated. Policies of "zero tolerance" and the search for a final solution to the drug problem have led us to support ineffective policies, to tolerate police practices that at times violate basic constitutional protections, and to crowd more and more people into the largest prison population in the "civilized" world (only Russia is the equal of the United States in the rate of incarceration; no other country is even close). Given recent policy developments, it is not difficult to imagine both welfare and drug policies evolving to the point where the routine acts of administrators could be directed at eliminating unwanted populations.

If any doubt remains about the capacity of Americans to create and even destroy a surplus population, consider the following two examples. First, General William C. Westmoreland described the North Vietnamese not as an enemy to be defeated but as "termites" to be exterminated by squashing them one by one, in the context of explaining the proper troop strength for the war effort:

> If you crowd in too many termite killers, each using a screwdriver to kill termites, you risk collapsing the floors or the foundation. In this war we're using screwdrivers to kill termites because it's a guerrilla war and we cannot use

bigger weapons. We have to get the right balance of termite killers to get rid of the termites without wrecking the house. (Stannard, 1992, pp. 252-253)

More than 20 years later, another American general, Norman Schwarzkopf, lamented the fact that he had been constrained in pursuing a war of annihilation in Iraq, even as American soldiers referred to killed Iraqi women and children as "collateral damage" and to the Iraqi people as "cockroaches" who ran for cover when the bombers appeared overhead (Stannard, 1992, p. 253).

Clearly, despite democratic traditions and rhetoric, Americans have the demonstrated capacity to engage in acts of administrative evil through public policies of destruction. In part, this stems from the tendency in American culture to absolve individuals from taking responsibility for their communities by framing social issues as problems that can and should be solved by experts, thereby ignoring the deeper, underlying conflicts that continue to tear away at the fabric of the culture. As discussed above, this can result in policies that create surplus populations. It also can lead us to abandon policies that, though not conforming to the image of a rational solution to a problem, represent an impulse to resist administrative evil and to create inclusive communities and workplaces, as well as more humane public policies.

Racism and Affirmative Action

Consider the policy of affirmative action as an approach to dealing with the problem of racial discrimination. Affirmative action had its roots in 1967 as a policy—the so-called Sullivan plan—that dealt specifically with the employment of African Americans (Farber, 1994). Designed to compensate for past discrimination, it addressed specifically the effects of racism against African Americans. Since then, affirmative action has been extended, or proposed for extension, to many other "protected classes" ("Affirmative Action," 1985).

Originally, the thought was that affirmative action would be necessary only for a limited number of years. It was thought of as the solution to past discrimination against a protected class (Goldman, 1976). Certainly, for example, after a generation of affirmative action and policies of non-discrimination, past discrimination begins to lose appeal as a claim. Part of the frustration with affirmative action stems from the fact that, like housing and welfare policies, it has not met the expectations of the technical-rational approach to problem solving. Opponents insist on knowing when the problem will be solved and affirmative action brought to an end. It is now clear that racism, in particular, is far more deeply embedded in American culture than we wanted to think (Hooks, 1993; Marable, 1995), and also that it would take many more years of affirmative action, at a minimum, to achieve a workforce that looks proportionally like the population at large.

Without in any way minimizing its real accomplishments—for actual gains have been achieved—it may not be an over-statement to observe that one of the main effects of affirmative action policies and programs has been to leave all parties with a feeling of being discriminated against, with affirmative action itself, like welfare, now viewed by some as a problem to be solved or eliminated (Bar-On, 1990). This is not a happy outcome, but at least part of the problem rests in how we have thought about affirmative action. African Americans, while generally strongly supportive of affirmative action, are not at all mystified about the relatively small gains achieved and the very large changes still to be made before they can think of their life chances, as a race, as anything beyond second class (Marable, 1995). On the other hand, once affirmative action is associated with preferential hiring, reverse discrimination, and/or quotas, Whites are negative toward it, and white males overwhelmingly so (Edsall & Edsall, 1991). Ironically, one outcome of this policy has been to deepen the racial divide.

Some have argued cogently that affirmative action simply has decreasing relevance for the problem of race in American culture (Massey, 1981, but see Carnoy, 1994). No one, for example, would be likely to argue any longer that affirmative action policies and programs have the transformative potential to reshape race relations in the United States, and certainly not without a dramatic widening of the scope of current policy and practice. Even if such a widening of scope could be justified, it seems politically infeasible in the current climate. This is not, however, a sufficient reason to abandon the affirmative action policies and programs that we currently have (O'Sullivan & Stewart, 1984). As in many other areas of social policy, it is quite possible to regress in race relations. (It is worth recalling here that the Holocaust occurred nearly a century after the political and legal emancipation of the Jews in Germany.) The point is that affirmative action no longer is advanced as a remedy for the broader and more crucial issue of racism in American culture (Farber, 1994).

One indication of the declining salience of affirmative action is the increasing problem of generating sufficiently large "qualified" pools of applicants from protected classes. A large pool of protected class applicants greatly aids successful affirmative action hiring. By the same token, a small pool makes it difficult to find an "equally qualified" protected class applicant, leaving essentially two poor choices—hiring an underqualified protected class applicant or, too often, business as usual. One response to this problem has been to question the relevance of the standards used to determine who is "qualified" (Webb & Liff, 1988). Critical race theory, arising largely from the law literature, argues that the standards should be revised from the perspective of the culture of the protected class (Farber, 1994, pp. 902-905). Essentially, they argue, we have a standards problem.

Others suggest that we have many prior problems to work on, having primarily to do with economic and educational inequality (Jencks, 1992). Black enrollment in colleges, for example, is either declining or flat, and because an undergraduate degree is a prerequisite for medical school admission, no amount of affirmative action can compensate for such shortfalls. An argument that a college degree (never mind the record of achievement) should not be a standard for medical school admission is not going to be persuasive, if anyone would even consider making such an argument. The powerful correlation between single-parent heads of household and poverty, race, and life chances, in terms of both income and education, also suggests that a broader view is needed (Fullinwider & Mills, 1986). Moreover, the American economy is changing in ways that further disadvantage African Americans; specifically, well-paid, low-skilled jobs are simply disappearing. This trend has been an important factor in the socially disastrous trends in labor force participation statistics for young African American males in particular, a group that has many of the characteristics of a surplus population.

Thus, in looking at some of the characteristics of affirmative action policies and programs, we are led to the more complex—and deeper—problem of racism in American culture. Racism and its associated issues are simply not susceptible to programmed solutions at the level of individuals; rather, these are structural, social problematics that require a constant, ongoing effort by a society committed to the well-being of all its members. Viewing affirmative action and other policies as problems to be solved, rather than recognizing the persistence of racism and the propensity to create and eliminate surplus populations, allows us both to blame others for not solving the problem (and thus avoid engagement with the more fundamental issues that divide our communities) and to sidestep the broader ethical dimensions of administrative action (Steinberg, 1994). The effort to eliminate affirmative action (and to force people off welfare) keeps alive the possibility that "in a multiethnic society the dominant ethnic majority might retain scarce jobs and resources for itself and eliminate competing minorities. That, in effect, is what the Germans did. We know to what extremes men with power can be driven under conditions of stress" (Rubenstein, 1975, p. 85).

Immigration Policy

We can see a similar, and equally serious, tendency to frame public policies in a way that creates surplus populations in the debate over immigration policy. For the most part, the problem is defined in terms of the impact of immigration on the economy and culture of the United States (Borjas, 1996; Kennedy, 1996). Those who support more open immigration policies point out how past immigrants have contributed to the economic and cultural development of the nation, and how the nation's future depends on our ability to fashion new ways to make immigrants part of our polity. Proponents of cracking down on illegal immigrants and limiting legal immigration maintain that immigrants will, at best, take jobs away from deserving Americans, or, at worst, become parasites dependent on welfare or crime. Thus it is argued (and made policy, for example, in California's Proposition 187) that public education, health benefits, and welfare ought to be denied to illegal and even to legal immigrants, with less consideration given to the nation's role in providing a safe haven for political refugees. The specter of a surplus population looms as unwanted peoples, including and even especially children and the elderly, are denied any legitimate role in society. Few seem to want to consider looking at the problems in a different way—for example, as stemming from the structure of the world economy and the practices of corporations that maximize profits by using low-wage labor and maintaining high unemployment in Third World countries.

Any debate over immigration policy should consider the historical record and the tragic consequences of past restrictions on immigration. The unwillingness of Congress to expand immigration of Jews from Europe in the 1930s stranded thousands of Jews who wanted to escape from Nazi Germany. Many of those denied entry to the United States and other countries eventually died in the Holocaust (Wyman, 1984). The ill-fated voyage of the *St. Louis* provides a case in point.

On May 13, 1939, the German liner *St. Louis* left Hamburg with 930 Jewish refugees. Of these, 734 held U.S. quota numbers, permitting entry into the United States within 3 years. All the refugees had Cuban landing certificates. En route to Havana, those on board the ship learned that Cuban authorities might question the "authenticity" of the landing certificates. On May 27, the *St. Louis* landed at Havana, but only 22 refugees were allowed off the ship. Five days later, Cuban authorities ordered the *St. Louis* to leave Cuban territorial waters. On June 3, the U.S. State Department rejected a proposal that the 734 refugees holding U.S. quota numbers be allowed to land in the United States. The *St. Louis* sailed slowly along the coast of Florida while efforts were made by U.S. Jews to offer the Cubans "financial guarantees" (bribes, really) of one million dollars; the Cubans rejected this and other overtures. On June 6, President Roosevelt received a telegram begging the United States to reconsider its refusal to provide a haven for these refugees. He failed to respond. After Chile, Paraguay, Argentina, and Colombia all refused asylum, the *St. Louis* returned to Europe. On June 11, the captain of the *St. Louis* considered beaching his ship on the English coast to prevent a return to Hamburg. The next day, Britain, Holland, and Belgium agreed to take the refugees, and they landed at Antwerp. The 624 who remained in Holland and Belgium came under Nazi occupation within a year; nearly all were transported to concentration camps. The 287 refugees who were accepted by Britain were interned as "enemy aliens" for a year after their admission, but they survived the war. If the story of the *St. Louis* reminds one of the more recent voyage of the garbage barge that was refused entry at every port of call on several continents, recall that the "cargo" of the *St. Louis* was human beings, but ones the Nazis had redefined as vermin.

The failure to provide leadership in this area, to send a message to Hitler that these people were valued members of the world community, confirmed in his mind the notion that the world did not care what happened to the Jews. By denying entry to Jewish refugees, the United States contributed to a world order in which the Jews were a surplus population and to their destruction by the Nazis. In the light of our poor performance earlier, we should be able to raise the question today: To what extent does our immigration policy contribute to a world order that impoverishes and exploits the very people who long to emigrate to our nation?

Operations Overcast and Paperclip

As we have seen, the von Braun team of German rocket scientists and engineers, more than 100 strong, were in the United States within a few months of the war's end. Under Operation Overcast, they had no problem in entering the country. This should not be surprising, because both Overcast and Paperclip were policies based on the goal of technical superiority. Achieving and maintaining superior technical expertise was simply a paramount goal for the United States, which as a country is certainly an exemplar of modernity. Nor should it be surprising that this end justified highly questionable means. We have been arguing all along that that is precisely a consequence of technical rationality. In spite of the fact that the Paperclip policy explicitly barred committed Nazis and even more obviously, war criminals, the end of technical superiority was all the justification needed by military intelligence officers and other public servants:

> German scientists and technicians were brought to the United States under a national policy that was developed and implemented by duly authorized, responsible agents of the U.S. government, including cabinet officers who consulted with and received the approval of the president. Under that national policy, the scientists were brought from Germany—either in disregard of or in violation of denazification procedures that the United States insisted on for other Germans. (Gimbel, 1990, p. 442)

Eli Pollach represents an interesting contrast to Arthur Rudolph and the rest of the von Braun team. Rudolph was included in the first Overcast wave in September, 1945; Pollach found himself in a displaced persons (DP) camp at that time. The DP camp was a great improvement over what preceded it. Pollach was a Hungarian Jew who was 17 years old when his entire family was transported to Auschwitz in late 1944. Pollach was the only one of his family to leave Auschwitz; he was transported to Dora, where he may well have seen, if only from a distance, Rudolph. Pollach spent those last months of the war on the V-2 assembly line at the Mittelwerk factory. After Pollach was liberated, it took him 4 years to get to the United States, in spite of the fact that he had relatives there (Hunt, 1991, p. 225). By that time, Rudolph and the von Braun team were moving to Huntsville, Alabama, and were settling into their new country quite nicely. Pollach did not think that the treatment afforded to

the von Braun team was just; however, he was still remark-
ably understanding, as illustrated in this quotation (Hunt,
1991, p. 226): "They have a saying in Hebrew, if you need
the thief, then you cut him off the gallows. But even if the
United States needed these scientists, they should have
reckoned a little bit for what they did."

With the benefit of hindsight, Operations Overcast and
Paperclip appear to be examples of administrative evil.
Although technical superiority has not disappeared as a
paramount American goal, even today, and although national security has been a valid rationale for many actions,
a justification for bringing committed Nazis and some individuals who were directly implicated in the use of SS slave
labor to the United States is not easily provided. The Cold
War provided an after-the-fact rationale for Paperclip, but at
the time, this was primarily an affirmative exercise—we
wanted this expertise for ourselves. The principle of denying
this expertise to others could easily have been met in other
ways. Rocket scientists who are incarcerated are not lending
their expertise to anyone else. There would have been plenty
of "clean" Germans to work on our rockets, and their lives
would not have been sullied by the knowledge and continuous anxiety of keeping the secret past. Arguably, we could
have done without the Germans altogether. For example,
there was a budding group of rocketeers at the Jet Propulsion
Laboratory in California (Neufeld, 1996). Granted, they were
years behind the Germans, but would it really have mattered
in the greater scheme of things if the moon landing occurred
in 1974 or even 1979? Our country did not need to land on
the moon carrying the symbolic baggage of 20,000 of Dora's
dead.

As Overcast and Paperclip and other policies have taught
us, we cannot afford to act as though individuals possess and
are protected by inherent human rights or by procedures and
laws. The illusion of rights that inhere in human nature and

each individual was smashed by the cold reality of the Holocaust, and it continues to be dispelled by the growing masses of surplus populations of the late 20th century. Individuals have rights and protections from oppressive policies only as members of a political community (Rubenstein, 1975, p. 89): "Outside of the polis there are no inborn restraints on the human exercise of destructive power." Administrative evil lurks where governments seek to solve social problems using the technical-rational expertise of professionals, in the absence of a vital and active political community. A new basis for ethics is needed that does not demand individual conformity to the procedures of technical-rational solutions to social problems, but that instead engages administrators as citizens in an ongoing effort to promote and sustain an inclusive democratic polity.

7

In the Face of Administrative Evil

Finding a Basis for Ethics in the Public Service

The modern world calls into existence certain concep-
tions of morality, but also destroys the grounds for taking
them seriously. Modernity both needs morality, and
makes it impossible.
                                    —*Ross Poole (1991, p. 261)*

Administrative evil poses a fundamental challenge to
the ethical foundations of public administration. Our
reluctance to recognize the importance of administrative evil
as part of the identity and practice of public administration
and public policy reinforces its continuing influence and
increases the possibility of future acts of dehumanization
and destruction in the name of the public interest. It is our
hope that this book will assist in finding a basis for ethics in
the public service, by unmasking administrative evil at least
to the extent of showing how it is inherent to modernity and
thus a part of the field's identity. The Holocaust and other
eruptions of administrative evil show that the assumptions
and standards for ethical behavior in modern, technical-

rational administrative systems are ultimately incapable of preventing or mitigating evil in either its subtle or its more obvious forms. With this final chapter, we suggest some positive steps toward adopting new ethical perspectives capable of helping public administrators avoid the hidden pathways and slippery slopes that lead into the abyss of administrative evil.

Necessary But Not Sufficient: The Legacy of the Technical-Rational Approach to Administrative Ethics

Ethics is the branch of philosophy concerned with systematic thought about character, morals, and "right action." In the modern age, until recently, two main versions of ethics have dominated Anglo-American philosophical thinking, namely teleological (or consequentialist) ethics and deontological ethics (Frankena, 1973). Both share an interest in determining the rules that should govern—and therefore be used to judge—individual behavior as good or bad, right or wrong. Teleological ethics, based on utilitarianism and tracing its lineage to Bentham (1789/1989) and others, offers the overarching principle of the greatest good for the greatest number. Oriented toward the results or consequences of actions, teleological ethics tends to elevate the ends over the means used to achieve those ends. Deontological ethics, founded in the thought of Kant (1959) and his support of duty and order, reverses this emphasis, holding that the lower-order rules governing means are essential for the higher-order rules that concern the ends to be achieved. For our purposes, the important point is that both of these traditions have focused on the individual as the relevant unit of analysis (Fox, 1991).

Ethics in the technical-rational tradition flows from the teleological tradition and focuses on the individual's decision-making process in the modern, bureaucratic organization and as a member of a profession. In the public sphere, ethics are meant to safeguard the integrity of the organization by helping individuals conform to professional norms, avoid mistakes and misdeeds that violate the public trust (corruption, nepotism, etc.), and ensure that public officials in a constitutional republic are accountable to the people through their elected representatives. In a constitutional order, public employees cannot be allowed to enrich themselves beyond their salaries or circumvent that order based on their individual interests or policy preferences.

It is fairly self-evident that public organizations depend on at least this level of ethical behavior to function efficiently and effectively, and to maintain public confidence in government. At the same time, it has to be recognized that these ethical standards of an organization or profession are only safeguards, and not fail-safes, against unethical behavior, nor do they necessarily help individuals to resolve tough moral dilemmas that often are characterized by ambiguity and paradox. Indeed, these problems provide the grist for the discourse among ethical theorists in the rational tradition. The Friedrich (1940)-Finer (1941) debate is still a useful way of describing the ethical terrain in public administration (Stewart, 1985b). Finer argued for a version of ethics that emphasized external standards and controls—laws, rules, regulations and codes. By contrast, Friedrich maintained that ethics was of necessity a matter of the individual's internal standards of conduct—a moral compass that would guide the public administrator through the morass of ethical dilemmas.

The Finer position of external controls is most compatible with a view of the public administrator as a neutral functionary who carries out, in Max Weber's phrase, *sine ira ac studio* (without bias or scorn), policy decisions made in the political sphere or by those in higher echelons of the organizational hierarchy. One author has gone so far as to argue that both an ethic of neutrality (decisions from politics) and an ethic of structure (decisions from higher up) preclude administrative ethics altogether because they deny the legitimacy of administrative discretion (Thompson, 1985; see also Ladd, 1970). The public administration literature on ethics has swung quite noticeably in the Friedrich direction (Fox & Cochran, 1990; see also Cooper, 1990) and now arguments in that literature are primarily over just which ethical grounds might justify administrative discretion. Prominent among the arguments for administrative discretion are (a) justice-based claims, usually following Rawls (Hart, 1984); (b) citizenship (Cooper, 1991); (c) American regime values (Rohr, 1978); (d) stewardship (Kass, 1990); (e) phronesis (Morgan, 1990); (f) conservation (Terry, 1995); and (g) countervailing responsibility (Harmon, 1995), among others.

In contemporary public administration, it has become almost an article of faith that professionalism imbues its practitioners with a public service ideal and a code of ethics—that is, internalized standards (after Friedrich) that provide the ethical compass for administrative discretion. To this way of thinking, professionalism becomes the basis for a version of virtue or character ethics (Stewart, 1985a; see also Cooper, 1987, and MacIntyre, 1984). On the other hand, professionalism also can offer a grounding for the external version of ethics (after Finer). Professions have codes of ethics, and they also often have some method of peer control, in which ethics and standards are enforced, and in the extreme, in which the serious transgressor can be drummed out of the profession (Kernaghan, 1980).

At the same time, most of the activity in the world of public administration practice has been directed at external controls. The promulgation of additional laws and regulations has dominated our response to the moral slough of the 1980s and 1990s, much as it did in the post-Watergate times. Foster (1981), among others, has called into question the common practice of equating law and ethics, or worse, substituting the former for the latter.

The depth and breadth within the public administration literature on ethics is to be applauded, yet it is unclear whether such theoretical formulations make an appreciable difference in the internal standards and norms of practicing administrators. Here the distinction suggested by Argyris (1990) between espoused theory and theory in use seems relevant. Espoused theory is, roughly, what we say we do and believe in, whereas theory in use stems from and informs actual behavior. Professional ethics appears in the public administration literature in both forms—espoused theory and theory in use (Pugh, 1989). At the level of espoused theory, one of the clearest associations of ethics and professionalism is found in an article by Kearney and Sinha:

> In a sense, the profession provides the professional administrator with a Rosetta Stone for deciphering and responding to various elements of the public interest. Professional accountability as embodied in norms and standards also serves as an inner check on an administrator's behavior. When joined with a code of ethics or conduct and the oath of office, professionalism establishes a value system that serves as a frame of reference for decision making, and creates a special form of social control conducive to bureaucratic responsiveness. (1988, p. 575)

In this view, the role model of professional expert technician fully satisfies the need for ethical standards in the modern organization. To be professional is to be ethical.

The Moral Vacuity
of Administrative Ethics

Despite the extensive literature in public administration ethics, there is little recognition of the most fundamental ethical challenge to the technical-rational approach to administrative ethics: that is, one can be a "good" or responsible administrator or professional and at the same time commit or contribute to acts of administrative evil. As Harmon (1995) has argued, technical-rational ethics has difficulty dealing with what Milgram (1974) termed the "agentic shift," in which the professional administrator acts responsibly toward the hierarchy of authority, public policy, and the requirements of the job or profession while abdicating any personal, much less social, responsibility for the content or effects of administrative actions. There is little in the way of coherent justification for the notion of a stable and predictable distinction between the individual's personal conscience guided by higher values that might resist the agentic shift, and the socialized administrator who internalizes agency values and obedience to legitimate authority. In the technical-rational conception of administrative ethics, the personal conscience is always subordinate to the structures of authority. The former is "subjective" and "personal," whereas the latter is characterized as "objective" and "public."

The specter of the agentic shift and the tightly controlled but soulless bureaucrat, along with the need for administrative discretion, helps explain why much of the recent literature in public administration ethics has leaned toward Friedrich's emphasis on internal control and personal conscience as the center of ethical behavior and standards. Some see this trend as leading to the usurping of democratic controls over public policy and a slippery slope toward government by bureaucracy (see Lowi, 1995).

This paradox is starkly illustrated in the Third Reich and the Holocaust. Many of the administrators directly responsible for the Holocaust were, from the technical-rational perspective, effective and responsible administrators who used administrative discretion to both influence and carry out the will of their superiors. Administrators such as Adolf Eichmann, Albert Speer, and Arthur Rudolph obeyed orders, followed proper protocol and procedures, and were often innovative and creative while carrying out their assigned tasks in an efficient and effective manner (Harmon, 1995; Hilberg, 1989; Keeley, 1983). Ironically, the SS was very concerned about corruption in its ranks and with strict conformance to the professional norms of its order (Sofsky, 1997).

As Rubenstein (1975) points out, no laws against genocide or dehumanization were broken by those who perpetrated the Holocaust. Everything was legally sanctioned and administratively approved by a legitimated authority, while at the same time, a number of key programs and innovations were initiated from within the bureaucracy (Browning, 1989; Sofsky, 1997). Even within the morally inverted universe created by the Nazis, administrators carried out their duties within a framework of ethics and responsibility that was consistent with the norms of technical-rational administration. The moral vacuity of administrative ethics is clearly revealed by the fact that the vast majority of those who participated in the Holocaust were never punished, and many were placed in responsible positions in postwar West German government or industry, as well as our own NASA and other public and private organizations in the United States. The need for "good" managers to rebuild the German economy and to develop our own rocket program outweighed any consideration of the administrative evil in which they were complicit.

The same emphasis on method and procedure that affected the political and administrative spheres also narrowed the conception of ethics within professionalism.
Hilberg (1989) points out that the professions were "every-
where" in the Holocaust. Lawyers, physicians, engineers,
planners, military professionals, accountants and more all
contributed to the destruction of the Jews and other "undesirables." Scientific methods were used in ways that dehu-
manized and murdered innocent human beings, showing
clearly how the model of professionalism consistent with
modernity drives out moral reasoning. Ethics became a chi-
merical accoutrement of professionalism, as it did in the
Tuskegee and nuclear materials experiments in the United
States, and as it did in Operations Overcast and Paperclip.

The historical record is such that we must conclude that
the power of the individual's conscience is very weak relative to that of legitimated authority in modern organizations
and social structures more generally, and that current ethical
standards do little or nothing to limit the potential for evil
in modern organizations. Even if the individual finds the
moral strength to resist administrative evil, the technical-
rational perspective provides little in the way of guidance for
how to act effectively against evil. As administrative ethics
is now construed, one cannot be a "civil servant" and be in
public disagreement with legally constituted political
authorities (Trow, 1997). A civil servant can voice disagreement with a public policy privately, but if this does not result
in a change of policy, the only acceptable courses of action
that remain are exit or loyalty (Harmon, 1995; Hirschman,
1970). One can resign and seek to change policy from the
outside (leaving only silent loyalists in the organization) or
remain and carry out the current policy. This was the choice
faced by German civil servants in the early 1930s, as
observed by Brecht (1944). If legitimate authority leads in
the direction of administrative evil, it will certainly not

provide legitimate outlets for resistance. In a situation of moral inversion, when duly constituted authority leads in the direction of evil, administrative ethics has no answers for the public servant.

Why, one might ask, does administrative ethics focus so much on the decision processes of the individual administrator at the expense of collective outcomes? Why is the individual conscience primarily responsible for ethical behavior, when it is political and managerial authority that are responsible for public policy and organizations? The answer is that operationally (theory in use), the central value is the primacy of legitimated authority. This is buttressed by the focus on the utility-maximizing individual as the locus of ethical decision making. In short, the ethical problem is construed as one of individual conformance to legitimate authority as a function of self-interest. The fact-value distinction (Simon, 1976) further separates the individual administrator from substantive judgments by limiting the field of ethical behavior to questions of efficiency and proper or innovative implementation of policy as determined by those who deal in the realm of values (policymakers). In effect, the ethical purview validated by technical rationality relieves, and even prohibits, individual administrators from making substantive value judgments.

Within the technical-rational tradition, there seems to be little or no room for allowing or encouraging civil servants to publicly disagree with policies that threaten the well-being of members of the polity, particularly policies that may produce or exploit surplus populations. Rather than expecting the individual civil servant to exit voluntarily when in serious disagreement with such public policies, public disagreement might press those in authority either to dismiss the offending administrator or to engage in a public debate over the policy. In either case, the policymakers would have to take responsibility for their policies, rather than place it on the shoulders of the administrators. One can only imagine whether things might have been different in Germany had the civil service spoken out against Nazi policies in the early days of the regime. True, individual civil servants would have done so at great personal risk, but, at the same time, the newly constituted government could not have sustained itself without their collective support. The fact that the vast majority of the German civil service felt that it had no choice but to conform once the legal basis for the new regime was established (Brecht, 1944), and that U.S. government scientists continued the Tuskegee experiments long after a cure for syphilis had been developed, along with numerous other examples, reveals how the ethical framework of technical-rational administration leaves little room for moral choice and resistance to administrative evil that is promoted by legitimate authority.

If the Holocaust teaches us anything, it is that individual administrators, far from resisting administrative evil, are most likely to be either helpless victims or willing accomplices. The ethical framework of modernity and its technical-rational ethos exalts the primacy of an abstract, utility-maximizing individual while binding administrators to bureaucratic organizations in ways that make them into reliable conduits for the dictates of legitimate authority, which is no less legitimate when it happens to be pursuing an evil policy. An ethical system that allows an individual to be a good administrator while committing acts of evil is necessarily devoid of moral content, or perhaps more accurately, morally perverse. When administrative evil can be unmasked, no public servant should be able to rest easy with the notion that ethical behavior is defined by doing things the right way. Norms of legality, efficiency, and effectiveness— however "professional" they may be—do not necessarily promote or protect the well-being of individuals, especially that of society's most vulnerable members.

Reconstructing a Public Ethics

The relationship between the individual and society has been a fundamental question of governance throughout the history of Western civilization. It has origins in the thought of the ancient Greeks, but it takes on particular significance with the political theory of Thomas Hobbes and John Locke in 17th-century England. For the first time in significant and sustained ways, the individual was set over and against society. Later, utilitarian philosophy (the base of teleological ethics) was articulated. In it, social welfare is seen as the aggregation of individual preferences.

Liberalism and democracy came together in the American founding period. A clear account of the marriage between liberalism and democracy appears in C. B. Macpherson's *The Life and Times of Liberal Democracy* (1977). The core values of classical liberalism are individualism, the notion of rights (particularly to property), the sanctity of contracts, and the rule of law. Classical liberalism sets the philosophical foundation for American society, which allows for and encourages differential achievement by individuals. Democracy's chief value—equality—often is outweighed within this framework. Americans of the founding period lived, as 20th-century Americans do, in an order fraught with the tension between the liberal and the democratic traditions.

Democratic principles were a driving force in the American Revolution (Countryman, 1985). Although political beliefs were widely divergent, there was widespread popular support for the democratic aims of the revolution; there had to be for the armies to be manned and for the struggle to be successfully pressed against the British. What lingers decisively, however, is not a polity based on the revolutionary rhetoric but instead the state that was built following the war during a time that has been appropriately called counter-revolutionary. The constitutional framework that was laid down during the founding period was formed far more from the principles of liberalism than from those of democracy. The core value of the more democratic, revolutionary period—equality—was given a severe reduction in rank by the Founding Fathers. The value of liberty—and the individual as its repository—was elevated and buttressed by law, by contract, and by right.

The American liberal democracy is thus predominantly procedural—civil liberties, voting, fair procedures in decision making, and technical-rational policy making (Adams et al., 1990). It is not designed to address the real conditions of people's lives that ultimately enable—or disallow—them to act as citizens in a democratic state. Equality itself has likewise been addressed predominantly in procedural terms; for example, equal employment opportunity has been operationalized through a variety of procedures. Those programs that most clearly address outcomes—for example, under an affirmative action policy, when an entity is mandated to hire members of a protected class until they constitute, say, 20% of all employees—generate the most resistance precisely because they conflict with the liberal values and procedural bias built into our political culture. Managing these tensions has been the great balancing act of liberal democracy in this country (Berlin, 1991). Arguably, however, it is the core value of individualism, married as it has been with technical rationality, that stands as a primary roadblock in finding a basis for public service ethics:

> The ambiguity and ambivalence of American individualism derive from both cultural and social contradictions. We insist, perhaps more than ever before, on finding our true selves independent of any cultural and social influence, being responsible to that self alone, and making its fulfillment the very meaning of our lives. Yet we spend much time navigating through immense bureaucratic structures—multiversities, corporation, government agencies—

manipulating and being manipulated by others. In describing this situation, Alasdair MacIntyre has spoken of "bureaucratic individualism." In bureaucratic individualism, the ambiguities and contradictions of individualism are frighteningly revealed, as freedom to make private decisions is bought at the cost of turning over most public decisions to bureaucratic managers and experts. A bureaucratic individualism in which the consent of the governed, the first demand of modern enlightened individualism, has been abandoned in all but form, illustrates the tendency of individualism to destroy its own conditions. (Bellah, Madsen, Sullivan, Swidler, & Tipton, 1985, p. 150)

Communitarianism, Citizenship, and Public Ethics

As the 20th century closes, two trends seem clear. First, interdependence is greater than it has ever been—people's fates are deeply intertwined—and this is less recognized than ever. Second, social groups are more and more fractionated and fractious—socially centripetal forces (racism perhaps chief among these) are as powerful as they have ever been, with more surplus populations appearing at the fringes of American society. Without the cohesion provided by a much greater sense of community, it is hard to see how American society can be kept from literally flying apart, except through coercive power and public policies of elimination, the most perversely tempting technical-rational solution to social and political disorder (Rubenstein, 1975, 1983). As a response to serious social fragmentation and economic dislocation, an authoritarian America now seems to be in the realm of the possible, one in which the barriers to "final solutions" seem likely to fall.

Given the centrality of relationships in the human condition, we have—whether we recognize it or not—the collective, shared experience from which arises the capacity to create and sustain human communities. We must literally "re-member" our appreciation of these multiple relations and renew our sense of obligation and responsibility within social settings. The challenge before us is a paradoxical one: We need to find or create a viable basis for the maintenance of legitimate public life even as there is less and less trust and tolerance for the constraints of political deliberation and decision (Saul, 1992). Out of this paradox must be created a new sense of responsibility and obligation toward public policies that seek to sustain communities rather than merely solve social problems. This is a daunting task, all the more so around issues of racism and surplus populations, but the American polity has reconstituted itself at more than one critical juncture in the past (Skowronek, 1982), although perhaps never so fundamentally and against such long odds.

Although "individualism lies at the very core of American culture" (Bellah et al., 1985, p. 142), the authors of *Habits of the Heart* found in their interviews a deep ambivalence about individualism and a recognition of the importance of community life:

> We found all the polarities of American individualism still operating: the deep desire for autonomy and self-reliance combined with an equally deep conviction that life has no meaning unless shared with others in the context of community; a commitment to the equal right to dignity of every individual combined with the effort to justify inequality of reward, which, when extreme, may deprive people of dignity; an insistence that life requires practical effectiveness and realism combined with the feeling that compromise is ethically fatal. The inner tensions of American individualism add up to a classic case of ambivalence. We strongly assert the value of our self-reliance and autonomy. We deeply feel the emptiness of a life without sustaining social commitments. Yet we are hesitant to articulate our sense that we need one another as much as we need to stand alone,

for fear that if we did we would lose our independence. (pp. 150-151)

This lingering attachment to community—that is, a communitarian political philosophy—has a long heritage in Western culture. Ancient (Aristotle), medieval (St. Thomas Aquinas), and modern (MacIntyre, 1984; Taylor, 1985) philosophers all have reflected communitarian politics and ethics. Various strands of communitarian thinking have appeared recently in the United States (Bellah, Madsen, Sullivan, Swidler, & Tipton, 1992; Chapman & Galston, 1992; Elshtain, 1990; Fishkin, 1991; McCollough, 1991; Spragens, 1990). These scholars believe, among other things, that a moral revival in the United States is possible without Puritanism or oppression, that people can again live in communities without turning into vigilantes or retreating to volkish enclaves, and that self-interest can be balanced by a commitment to the community without requiring austerity, altruism, or self-sacrifice (Etzioni, 1993, pp. 1-2), all of which represent important and ongoing challenges to any communitarian enterprise (Fox & Miller, 1994).

Across a variety of public policy issues, communitarian proposals emphasize rejuvenated social obligations, activities that strengthen communities (Etzioni, 1991). In the area of family policy, for example, communitarians tend to promote initiatives that would reduce the "parenting deficit," such as more liberal family leave policies that enable parents to spend more time with (that is, meet their responsibility to) very young children (Etzioni, 1993, Chapter 2). The area of family policy also includes a variety of initiatives to reduce "entertainment violence," which increasingly dominates all areas of television programming, including "news" (as a journalists' saying goes, "if it bleeds, it leads"). One of the better-known policy initiatives of communitarians is the idea of voluntary or even mandatory national service for young people of high school or college age. A 1- or 2-year public service experience, it is thought, could instill a lifetime appreciation for community and might be rewarded, for example, by tuition credits for further education. This proposal is seen as an unwarranted infringement on individual liberty by many.

These are promising policy initiatives, and there are many others (Barber, 1993; Yankelovich, 1991). The introduction of new policies, even the introduction of new values, into the political arena and into social discourse is not sufficient by itself, however, to alter the American social and political landscape. A more fundamental rethinking is a prerequisite to the kind of social change needed to address the potential for administrative evil and policies of destruction inherent in modern civilization. The communitarians refer to it as a "change of heart."

Communitarian ethics (also known as neo-Aristotelian, character, or virtue ethics) offers a possible alternative to the technical-rational approach to administrative ethics and the associated complex of problems associated with administrative evil. Alasdair MacIntyre (1984) provided the groundbreaking work within this literature. Communitarians do not locate ethics in the autonomous individual, but within the community. That is, ethics emerges from the relational context within which people act—within the public square. This perspective has major implications for governance and administration in a democratic polity.

Communitarians favor a strong democracy, where "we seek to make government more representative, more participatory, and more responsive to all members of the community. We seek to find ways to accord citizens more information and more say, more often" (Etzioni, 1993, p. 253). In this view of democracy, the practice of ethics and the practice of politics are not separated as in the technical-rational approach, but are mutually entailing. That is, the process of building a community—in this case, not just a political community, but an inclusive, democratic community—develops public life and public ethics at the same time. As detailed by Deborah Stone (1988), a political community has the following characteristics:

- It is a community.
- It has a public interest, if only an idea about which people will fight.
- Most of its policy problems are common problems.
- Influence is pervasive, and the boundary between influence and coercion is always contested.
- Cooperation is as important as competition.
- Loyalty is the norm.
- Groups and organizations are the building blocks.
- Information is interpretive, incomplete, and strategic.
- It is governed by the laws of passion as well as of matter.
- Power, derivative of all those elements, coordinates individual intentions and actions into collective purposes and results. (p. 25)

Publicness is a key aspect in this development, as Ventriss (1993, p. 201) notes: "A public, therefore, is a community of citizens who attempt to understand the substantive interdependency of social and political issues on the community, and who maintain a critical perspective on the ethical implications of governmental policy making." In this view, it would be unethical for public servants *not* to speak publicly to policy issues. As citizen administrators in a democratic community, they would have a special responsibility to guard against policies and practices that might engender eruptions of administrative evil.

This critical and active citizenship is a key aspect of building a viable democracy. Camilla Stivers (1993) has articulated the following characteristics of democratic citizenship:

- The exercise of authoritative power, using sound judgment and relying on practical knowledge of the situation at hand.
- The exercise of virtue, or concern for the public interest, defined substantively in particular contexts through reasoned discourse.
- The development of personal capacities for governance through their exercise in practical activity.
- The constitution of community through deliberation about issues of public concern. (p. 441)

In Stivers's view, active citizenship means participation in governance and the exercise of decisive judgment in the public interest, an experience that develops the political and moral capacities of individuals and solidifies the communal ties among them.

A communitarian approach to democratic governance clearly makes demands on individuals, and on individuals acting together in the public interest. It views exclusion and nonparticipation in public life as major problems in and of themselves. Public policies based on exclusion and exploitation are entirely inimical to a communitarian democracy because they "weaken the community by undermining the civic bonds that unify it, while eroding the political process by converting what should be a dialogue between fellow citizens into a repressive hierarchy" (Farber, 1994, p. 929). This is precisely what occurred in Nazi Germany. Under the rhetoric of a unified community, the Nazis' racist and exclusionary policies created a polity held together not by civic bonds but by the terror of the concentration camps (Goldhagen, 1996; Sofsky, 1997).

Procedural democracy, which may open doors to individuals through policies like affirmative action, can provide formal access to excluded or marginalized groups. Formal access, however, offers no guarantee, and indeed little enough prospect, of full participation in the community—the sort of active citizenship described above. Liberal democracy, largely through its liberal side, places its major emphasis on the *rights* of individuals; communitarian democracy can be built only on a foundation of *responsibilities* and the hard work of citizenship. Policies and social programs, such as those related to affirmative action, welfare, public housing, immigration, and illicit drugs, would be judged on the basis of their effectiveness in building community and on administrators' success in involving citizens in policy making and implementation (see, for example, Balfour and Smith, 1996).

The hard work of citizenship suggests one more aspect of liberal democracy that impedes public life and public ethics. The granting of procedural rights, although important in its own regard, fails to address the substantive conditions— usually economic and social—that enable or disable a citizen's engagement in public life. As Stivers (1993, p. 452) puts it, "the granting of formal rights fails to create the conditions under which all citizens are able to order their lives to attain the minimally adequate level of comfort and security that would make their participation in political life possible and meaningful." For example, the poverty rate among all families in the United States in 1993 was 15%; for female head of household families the rate was 39%; and for families with a black female head of household the rate was an incredible 53%. For a family with a female head of household, the simple availability of child care is just the beginning of a series of obstacles that confront the willing-to-participate citizen. It is well known that both registration and voting rates drop with the level of income. The burdens of poverty crush even the exercise of minimum procedural rights such as voting and certainly extinguish the more extensive responsibilities of "active" citizenship. The social burden of race (see Ashe, 1993) exacerbates all these difficulties.

A public ethics for public administration would require that administrators be attentive to social and economic outcomes of public policy, as well as to their proper and faithful implementation. Public administrators could not ethically implement a policy that was overtly detrimental to the well-being of any segment of the population. It would be unethical, for example, to cooperate with cutting off disability benefits to legal immigrants, many of whom are elderly and are likely to wind up malnourished and/or homeless. Such a policy amounts to defining this group as a surplus population, and an ethical public service cannot be complicit in that sort of public policy.

Strong communities—even strong, democratic communities—offer no guarantees against administrative evil. They certainly offer no escape from evil itself, which remains a part of the human condition. Still, administrative evil may not be so easily masked in strong, democratic communities, and public servants do not so easily wear the mask of administrative evil when their role entails a critically reflexive sense of the context of public affairs along with a mission to educate and build an inclusive and active citizenry. Unmasking administrative evil offers no easy or sentimental solutions and offers no promise of making anything better; it offers only an inevitably small and fragile bulwark against things going really wrong—those genuinely horrific eruptions of evil that modernity has exacerbated very nearly beyond our willingness to comprehend. Raul Hilberg recalls a statement made by Sigmund Freud in Vienna in the 1920s:

> Do not despair. You need not worry so much about the future of civilization, for mankind has not yet risen so far, that he has so very far to fall.

References

Adam, U. D. (1989). The gas chambers. In F. Furet (Ed.), *Unanswered questions: Nazi Germany and the genocide of the Jews* (pp. 134-154). New York: Schocken.

Adams, G. B., Bowerman, P. V., Dolbeare, K. M., & Stivers, C. (1990). Joining purpose to practice: A democratic identity for the public service. In H. D. Kass & B. L. Catron (Eds.), *Images and identities in public administration* (pp. 219-240). Newbury Park, CA: Sage.

Adams, G. B., & Ingersoll, V. (1990). Culture, technical rationality and organizational culture. *American Review of Public Administration, 20,* 285-302.

Adams, M. M., & Merrihew, R. (Eds.). (1990). *The problem of evil.* New York: Oxford University Press.

Affirmative action: Past, present, and future [Symposium]. (1985). *American Behavioral Scientist, 28.*

Alford, F. C. (1990). The organization of evil. *Political Psychology, 11,* 5-27.

Allcorn, S., & Diamond, M. A. (1997). *Managing people during stressful times: The psychologically defensive workplace.* Westport, CT: Quorum.

Allen, W. H. (1907). *Efficient democracy.* New York: Dodd and Mead.

Allison, G. T. (1971). *The essence of decision: Explaining the Cuban Missile Crisis.* Glenview, IL: Scott, Foresman.

Anna, H. J. (1976). *Task groups and linkages in complex organizations: A case study of NASA.* Beverly Hills, CA: Sage.

Arad, Y., Gutman, Y., & Margaliot, A. (Eds.). (1981). *Documents in the Holocaust.* New York: Pergamon.

Arendt, H. (1954). *Between past and future.* Cleveland: World Publishing.

Arendt, H. (1958). *The origins of totalitarianism.* Cleveland: Meridian.

Arendt, H. (1963). *Eichmann in Jerusalem: A report on the banality of evil.* New York: Viking.

Argyris, C. (1990). *Overcoming organizational defenses.* Reading, MA: Addison-Wesley.

Aronson, S. H. (1964). *Status and kinship in the higher civil service.* Cambridge, MA: Harvard University Press.

Ashe, A. (1993). *Days of grace: A memoir.* New York: Alfred A. Knopf.

Balfour, D. L., & Smith, J. L. (1996). Transforming lease-purchase housing programs for low income families: Towards empowerment and engagement. *Journal of Urban Affairs, 18*(2), 173-188.

Barber, B. R. (1993). *An aristocracy of everyone: The politics of education and the future of America.* New York: Oxford University Press.

Barley, S. R., Meyer, G. W., & Gash, D. C. (1988). Cultures of culture: Academics, practitioners and the pragmatics of normative control. *Administrative Science Quarterly, 33,* 24-60.

Bar-On, D. (1990). Discrimination, individual justice, and preferential treatment. *Public Affairs Quarterly, 4,* 111-137.

Barrett, W. (1979). *The illusion of technique.* Garden City, NY: Anchor Doubleday.

Bauman, Z. (1989). *Modernity and the Holocaust.* Ithaca, NY: Cornell University Press.

Baumeister, R. F. (1997). *Evil: Inside human cruelty and violence.* New York: W. H. Freeman.

Bellah, R. N. (1971). Evil and the American ethos. In A. Nevitt & C. Comstock (Eds.), *Sanctions for evil* (pp. 177-191). San Francisco: Jossey-Bass.

Bellah, R. N., Madsen, R., Sullivan, W. R., Swidler, A., & Tipton, S. M. (1985). *Habits of the heart: Individualism and commitment in American life.* New York: Harper and Row.

Bellah, R. N., Madsen, R., Sullivan, W. R., Swidler, A., & Tipton, S. M. (1992). *The good society.* New York: Alfred A. Knopf.

Bellush, J., & Hausknecht, M. (Eds.). (1967). *Urban renewal: People, politics and planning.* Garden City, NY: Doubleday Anchor.

Bendix, R. (1956). *Work and authority in industry.* New York: Harper and Row.

Bentham, J. (1989). *Vice and virtue in everyday life.* New York: Harcourt, Brace, Jovanovich. (Original work published 1789)

Beon, Y. (1997). *Planet Dora: A memoir of the Holocaust and the birth of the space age.* Boulder, CO: Westview.

Berenbaum, M. (1993). *The world must know.* Boston: Little, Brown, & Company.

Berger, P. L., & Luckmann, T. (1967). *The social construction of reality.* Garden City, NY: Doubleday.

Berlin, I. (1991). *The crooked timber of humanity.* New York: Alfred A. Knopf.

Bernstein, R. (Ed.). (1985). *Habermas and modernity.* Cambridge, MA: MIT Press.

Bilstein, R. E. (1980). *Stages to Saturn: A technological history of the Apollo/Saturn launch vehicles.* Washington, DC: National Aeronautics and Space Administration.

Blanco, H. (1994). *How to think about social problems.* Westport, CT: Greenwood.

Bok, S. (1978). *Lying: Moral choice in public and private life.* New York: Vintage.

Borjas, G. J. (1996, November). The new economics of immigration. *The Atlantic Monthly,* pp. 72-80.

Bower, T. (1987). *The Paperclip conspiracy.* London: Michael Joseph.

Brecht, A. (1944). *Prelude to silence.* New York: Oxford University Press.

Breton, A., & Wintrobe, R. (1986). The bureaucracy of murder revisited. *Journal of Political Economy, 94,* 905-926.

Brooks, C. G., Grimwood, J. M., & Swenson, L. S., Jr. (1979). *Chariots for Apollo.* Washington, DC: National Aeronautics and Space Administration.

Broszat, M. (1981). *The Hitler state: The foundation and development of the internal structure of the Third Reich.* London: Longman.

Browning, C. R. (1980). The government experts. In H. Friedlander & S. Milton (Eds.), *The Holocaust: Ideology, bureaucracy and genocide* (pp. 183-198). Millwood, NY: Kraus International Publications.

Browning, C. (1983). The German bureaucracy and the Holocaust. In A. Grobman & D. Landes (Eds.), *Genocide: Critical issues of the Holocaust* (pp. 145-149). Los Angeles: Simon Wiesenthal Center.

Browning, C. (1989). The decision concerning the final solution. In F. Furet (Ed.), *Unanswered questions: Nazi Germany and the genocide of the Jews* (pp. 96-118). New York: Schocken.

Browning, C. (1992). *The path to genocide.* Cambridge, UK: Cambridge University Press.

Caiden, G. E. (1984). In search of an apolitical science of American public administration. In J. Rabin & J. S. Bowman (Eds.), *Politics and administration: Woodrow Wilson and American public administration* (pp. 51-76). New York: Marcel Dekker.

Caldwell, L. K. (1976). Novus Ordo Seclorum: The heritage of American public administration. *Public Administration Review, 36,* 476-488.

Caldwell, L. K. (1990). The administrative republic: The contrasting legacies of Hamilton and Jefferson. *Public Administration Quarterly, 3,* 470-493.

Carnoy, M. (1994). *Faded dreams: The politics and economics of race in America.* New York: Cambridge University Press.

Chandler, R. C. (Ed.). (1987). *A centennial history of the American administrative state.* New York: Free Press.

Chapman, J. W., & Galston, W. A. (Eds.). (1992). *Virtue.* New York: New York University Press.

Chapman, R. L. (1973). *Project management at NASA: The system and the men.* Washington, DC: National Aeronautics and Space Administration.

Charney, I. W. (1984). *Toward the understanding and prevention of genocide.* Boulder, CO: Westview.

Christensen, K. S. (1985). Coping with uncertainty in planning. *Journal of the American Planning Association, 51,* 63-73.

Committee on Science and Technology. (1986). *Investigation of the Challenger accident: Hearings before the Committee on Science and Technology* (2 vols.). Washington, DC: U.S. House of Representatives.

Cook, R. (1986, November). The Rogers Commission failed: Questions it never asked, answers it didn't listen to. *The Washington Monthly,* pp. 13-21.

Cooper, T. L. (1987). Hierarchy, virtue and the practice of public administration: A perspective for normative ethics. *Public Administration Review, 47,* 320-328.

Cooper, T. L. (1990). *The responsible administrator.* San Francisco: Jossey-Bass.

Cooper, T. L. (1991). *An ethic of citizenship for public administration.* Englewood Cliffs, NJ: Prentice Hall.

Countryman, E. (1985). *The American Revolution.* New York: Hill and Wang.

Croly, H. (1909). *The promise of American life.* New York: Macmillan.

Cuff, R. D. (1978). Wilson and Weber: Bourgeois critics in an organized age. *Public Administration Review, 38,* 240-244.

Dawidowicz, L. (1975). *The war against the Jews, 1933-1945.* New York: Holt, Rinehart and Winston.

Delbanco, A. (1995). *The death of Satan: How Americans have lost the sense of evil.* New York: Farrar Strauss and Giroux.

Delbecq, A. L., & Filley, A. (1974). *Program and project management in a matrix organization: A case study.* Madison: Bureau of Business Research and Service, University of Wisconsin–Madison.

Diamond, M. A. (1988). Organizational identity: A psychoanalytic exploration of organizational meaning. *Administration and Society, 20,* 166-190.

Diamond, M. A. (1993). *The unconscious life of organizations: Interpreting organizational identity.* Westport, CT: Quorum.

Dietrich, D. J. (1981). Holocaust as public policy: The Third Reich. *Human Relations, 34,* 445-462.

Dwork, D., & van Pelt, R. J. (1996). *Auschwitz: 1270 to the present.* New York: Norton.

Edelheit, H., & Edelheit, A. J. (1991). *A world in turmoil: An integrated chronology of the Holocaust and World War II.* New York: Greenwood.

Edelman, M. J. (1977). *Political language: Words that succeed and policies that fail.* New York: Academic Press.

Edsall, T. B., & Edsall, M. D. (1991). *Chain reaction: The impact of face, rights and taxes on American politics.* New York: Norton.

Eliot, G. (1972). *The twentieth century book of the dead.* New York: Scribner.

Ellul, J. (1954). *The technological society.* New York: Vintage.

Elshtain, J. B. (1990). *Power trips and other journeys.* Madison: University of Wisconsin Press.

Ely, R. (1982). Report of the organization of the American Economic Association, 1986. In M. B. Levy (Ed.), *Political thought in America: An anthology* (pp. 282-285). Homewood, IL: Dorsey.

Etzioni, A. (1991). *A responsive society.* San Francisco: Jossey-Bass.

Etzioni, A. (1993). *The spirit of community: Rights, responsibilities, and the communitarian agenda.* New York: Crown.

Farber, D. A. (1994). The outmoded debate over affirmative action. *California Law Review, 82,* 893-934.

Faulconer, J. E., & Williams, R. N. (1985). Temporality in human action: An alternative to positivism and historicism. *American Psychologist, 40,* 1179-1188.

Fein, H. (1979). *Accounting for genocide: National responses and Jewish victimization during the Holocaust.* New York: Free Press.

Finer, H. (1941). Administrative responsibility in democratic government. *Public Administration Review, 1,* 335-350.

Fishkin, J. S. (1991). *Democracy and deliberation.* New Haven, CT: Yale University Press.

FitzGibbon, C. (1969). *Denazification.* London: Michael Joseph.

Follett, M. P. (1918). *The new state.* New York: Longmans.

Foster, G. D. (1981). Law, morality and the public servant. *Public Administration Review, 41,* 29-34.

Fox, C. J. (1991). *Nomothetic decision making in public administration ethics: A critique, a recommendation and a pedagogical suggestion.* Unpublished manuscript, Texas Tech University, Lubbock, TX.

Fox, C. J., & Cochran, C. E. (1990). Discretionary public administration: Toward a platonic guardian class. In H. J. Kass & B. L. Catron (Eds.), *Images and identities in public administration* (pp. 87-112). Newbury Park, CA: Sage.

Fox, C. J., & Miller, H. T. (1994). *Postmodern public administration: Toward discourse.* Thousand Oaks, CA: Sage.

Frankena, W. (1973). *Ethics* (2nd ed.). Englewood Cliffs, NJ: Prentice Hall.

Frederickson, H. G. (1980). *The new public administration.* University: University of Alabama Press.

Frederickson, H. G., & Hart, D. K. (1985). The public service and the patriotism of benevolence. *Public Administration Review, 45,* 547-553.

Friedlander, S. J. (1997). *Nazi Germany and the Jews: Vol. 1. The years of persecution.* New York: HarperCollins.

Friedrich, C. J. (1940). Public policy and the nature of administrative responsibility. In C. J. Friedrich & E. S. Mason (Eds.), *Public policy* (pp. 221-245). Cambridge, MA: Harvard University Press.

Fullinwider, R. K., & Mills, C. (1986). *The moral foundation of civil rights.* Totowa, NJ: Rowman and Littlefield.

Garlinski, J. (1978). *Hitler's last weapons: The underground war against the V1 and V2.* New York: Times Books.

Gimbel, J. (1986). U.S. policy and German scientists: The early Cold War. *Political Science Quarterly, 101,* 433-451.

Gimbel, J. (1990). German scientists, United States denazification policy and the "Paperclip conspiracy." *International History Review, 12,* 441-485.

Glass, J. M. (1997). *"Life unworthy of life": Racial phobia and mass murder in Hitler's Germany.* New York: Basic Books.

Goldhagen, D. J. (1996). *Hitler's willing executioners: Ordinary Germans and the Holocaust.* New York: Alfred A. Knopf.

Goldman, A. H. (1976). Affirmative action. *Philosophy and Public Affairs, 5,* 178-195.

Graebner, W. (1987). *The engineering of consent: Democracy and authority in twentieth century America.* Madison: University of Wisconsin Press.

Graham, J. F. (1995). *History of Apollo and Saturn.* Washington, DC: National Aeronautics and Space Administration.

Green, R. T. (1990). Alexander Hamilton and the study of public administration. *Public Administration Quarterly, 13,* 494-514.

Greenberg, J., & Mitchell, S. (1983). *Object relations in psychoanalytic theory.* Cambridge, MA: Harvard University Press.

Guerreiro-Ramos, A. (1981). *The new science of organization.* Toronto: University of Toronto Press.

Haber, S. (1964). *Efficiency and uplift: Scientific management in the Progressive Era, 1890-1920.* Chicago: University of Chicago Press.

Haney, C., Banks, C., & Zimbardo, P. (1974). Interpersonal dynamics in a simulated prison. *International Journal of Criminology and Penology, 1*, 69-97.

Hanson, R. L. (1985). *The democratic imagination in America: Conversations with our past.* Princeton, NJ: Princeton University Press.

Harmon, M. M. (1995). *Responsibility as paradox: A critique of rational discourse on government.* Thousand Oaks, CA: Sage.

Hart, D. K. (1984). The virtuous citizen, the honorable bureaucrat and "public" administration. *Public Administration Review, 44*, 111-120.

Hegel, G.W.F. (1965). Preface to the phenomenology of mind. In W. Kaufman (Ed.), *Hegel: Texts and commentary* (pp. 1-112). Notre Dame, IN: Notre Dame University Press. (Original work published 1807)

Heidegger, M. (1977). *Basic writings.* New York: Harper and Row. (Original work published 1926)

Henry, N. (1990). Root and branch: Public administration's travail toward the future. In N. Lynn & A. Wildavsky (Eds.), *Public administration: State of the discipline* (pp. 3-26). Chatham, NJ: Chatham House.

Herrnstein, R., & Murray, C. (1994). *The bell curve.* New York: Free Press.

Higgs, R. (1987). *Crisis and Leviathan: Critical episodes in the growth of American government.* New York: Oxford University Press.

Hilberg, R. (1985). *The destruction of the European Jews* (3rd ed.). New York: Holmes & Meier.

Hilberg, R. (1989). The bureaucracy of annihilation. In F. Furet (Ed.), *Unanswered questions: Nazi Germany and the genocide of the Jews* (pp. 119-133). New York: Schocken.

Hirsch, H. (1995). *Genocide and the politics of memory.* Chapel Hill: University of North Carolina Press.

Hirschman, A. (1970). *Exit, voice and loyalty.* Cambridge, MA: Harvard University Press.

Hofstadter, R. (1955). *The age of reform.* New York: Vintage.

Hoogenboom, A. A. (1961). *Outlawing the spoils: A history of the civil service reform movement.* Urbana: University of Illinois Press.

Hooks, B. (1993). *Killing rage: Ending racism.* New York: Henry Holt.

Horkheimer, M. (1947). *The eclipse of reason.* New York: Oxford University Press.

Horowitz, I. L. (1980). *Taking lives: Genocide and state power.* New Brunswick, NJ: Transaction Books.

Houston, D. J., & Delevan, S. M. (1990). Public administration research: An assessment of journal publications. *Public Administration Review, 50*, 674-681.

Hummel, R. (1987). *The bureaucratic experience* (3rd ed.). New York: St. Martin's.

Hunt, L. (1991). *Secret agenda: The United States government, Nazi scientists, and Project Paperclip.* New York: St. Martin's.

Hunter, D. H. (1991). *Culture wars: The struggle to define America.* New York: Basic Books.

Huxley, A. (1948). *Ape and essence.* New York: Harper and Brothers.

Huxley, A. (1952). *The devils of Loudon.* New York: Harper and Row.

Irving, D. C. (1965). *The mare's nest.* Boston: Brown.

Jencks, C. (1992). *Rethinking social policy: Race, poverty and the underclass.* Cambridge, MA: Harvard University Press.

Kant, I. (1959). *Metaphysical foundations of morals.* Indianapolis, IN: Bobbs-Merrill.

Karl, B. D. (1974). *Charles E. Merriam and the study of politics.* Chicago: University of Chicago Press.

Karl, B. D. (1976). Public administration and American history: A century of professionalism. *Public Administration Review, 36,* 489-504.

Karl, B. D. (1987). The American bureaucrat: A history of a sheep in wolves' clothing. *Public Administration Review, 47,* 26-34.

Kass, H. D. (1990). Stewardship as a fundamental element in images of public administration. In H. D. Kass & B. L. Catron (Eds.), *Image and identity in public administration* (pp. 113-131). Newbury Park, CA: Sage.

Kass, H. D., & Catron, B. L. (Eds.). (1990). *Image and identity in public administration.* Newbury Park, CA: Sage.

Kateb, G. (1983). *Hannah Arendt, politics, conscience, evil.* Totowa, NJ: Rowman & Allanheld.

Katz, F. E. (1993). *Ordinary people and extraordinary evil: A report on the beguilings of evil.* Albany: State University of New York Press.

Katz, J. (1988). *Seductions of crime: Moral and sensual attractions in doing evil.* New York: Basic Books.

Katz, M. B. (1989). *The undeserving poor: From the war on poverty to the war on welfare.* New York: Pantheon.

Kearney, R. C., & Sinha, C. (1988). Professionalism and bureaucratic responsiveness: Conflict or compatibility. *Public Administration Review, 48,* 571-579.

Keeley, M. (1983). Values in organizational theory and management education. *Academy of Management Review, 8*(3), 376-386.

Kekes, J. (1990). *Facing evil.* Princeton, NJ: Princeton University Press.

Keller, D. F. (1985). *Reflections on gender and science.* New Haven, CT: Yale University Press.

Kelman, H. C., & Hamilton, V. (1989). *Crimes of obedience: Toward a social psychology of authority and responsibility.* New Haven, CT: Yale University Press.

Kennedy, D. M. (1996, November). Can we still afford to be a nation of immigrants? *The Atlantic Monthly,* pp. 52-68.

Kennedy, G. P. (1983). *Vengeance weapon 2.* Washington, DC: Smithsonian Institution Press.

Kerlinger, F. N. (1964). *Foundations of behavioral research.* New York: Holt, Rinehart and Winston.

Kernaghan, K. (1980). Codes of ethics and public administration. *Public Administration, 59,* 207-223.

Klee, E., Dressen, W., & Riess, V. (Eds.). (1991). *The Holocaust as seen by its perpetrators and bystanders.* New York: Free Press.

Klee, E., & Merk, O. (1965). *The birth of the missile: The secrets of Peenemünde.* New York: Dutton.

Klein, M. (1964). *Love, hate and reparation.* New York: Free Press.

Kolko, G. (1963). *The triumph of conservatism: A reinterpretation of American history, 1900-1916.* New York: Free Press.

Kuper, L. (1981). *Genocide: Its political use in the twentieth century.* New Haven, CT: Yale University Press.

Ladd, J. (1970). Morality and the ideal of rationality in organizations. *The Monist, 54,* 488-516.

Lael, S. A., & Marcus, P. (Eds.). (1984). *Psychoanalytic reflections on the Holocaust.* New York: Ktav.

Lang, B. (1991). The history of evil and the future of the Holocaust. In P. Hayes (Ed.), *Lessons and legacies: The meaning of the Holocaust in a changing world* (pp. 90-105). Evanston, IL: Northwestern University Press.

Larson, M. L. (1977). *The rise of professionalism.* Berkeley: University of California Press.

Lasby, C. G. (1971). *Project Paperclip: German scientists and the Cold War.* New York: Atheneum.

Levine, A. S. (1982). *Managing NASA in the Apollo era.* Washington, DC: National Aeronautics and Space Administration.

Lindbergh, C. A. (1978). *Autobiography of values.* New York: Harcourt, Brace, Jovanovich.

Link, A. S. (1964). *Woodrow Wilson and the Progressive Era, 1910-1917.* New York: Harper and Row.

Lippman, M. (1995). War crimes: American prosecution of Nazi military officers. *Touro International Law Review, 6,* 243-276.

Lipton, R. J. (1986). *The Nazi doctors: Medical killing and the psychology of genocide.* New York: Basic Books.

Lowi, T. J. (1995). *The end of the republican era.* Norman: University of Oklahoma Press.

Lustig, R. J. (1982). *Corporate liberalism: The origin of modern American political theory, 1890-1920.* Berkeley: University of California Press.

Lynn, L. E., Jr. (1996). *Public management as art, science, and profession.* Chatham, NJ: Chatham House.

Machiavelli, N. (1961). *The prince.* London: Penguin. (Original work published c. 1520)

MacIntyre, A. (1981). *After virtue.* Notre Dame, IN: University of Notre Dame Press.

MacIntyre, A. (1984). *After virtue* (2nd ed.). Notre Dame, IN: Notre Dame University Press.

Macpherson, C. B. (1977). *The life and times of liberal democracy.* New York: Oxford University Press.

Mannheim, K. (1940). *Man and society in an age of reconstruction.* New York: Harcourt, Brace and World.

Marable, M. (1995). *Beyond black and white: Transforming African-American politics.* New York: Verso.

Marini, F. (Ed.). (1971). *Toward a new public administration.* Scranton, PA: Chandler.

Marshall, G. S., & White, O. F., Jr. (1990). The Blacksburg Manifesto and the postmodern debate: Public administration in a time without a name. *American Review of Public Administration, 20,* 61-76.

Mason, T. (1981). Intention and explanation: A current controversy about the interpretation of National Socialism. In A. Hirschfeld & L. Kettenacker (Eds.), *Der Führerstaat: Mythos und Realität* [The "Führer State": Myth and reality] (pp. 21-40). Stuttgart: Klett-Cotta.

Massey, S. J. (1981). Rethinking affirmative action. *Social Theory and Practice, 7,* 21-47.

McCollough, T. E. (1991). *The moral imagination and public life.* Chatham, NJ: Chatham House.

McConnell, M. (1987). *Challenger: A major malfunction.* New York: Doubleday.

McCurdy, H. E. (1993). *Inside NASA: High technology and organizational change in the U.S. space program.* Baltimore: Johns Hopkins University Press.

McCurdy, H. E.,. & Cleary, R. E. (1984). Why can't we resolve the research issue in public administration? *Public Administration Review, 44,* 49-56.

McGovern, J. (1964). *Crossbow and overcast.* New York: W. Morrow.

McSwite, O. C. (1997). *Legitimacy in public administration: A discourse analysis.* Thousand Oaks, CA: Sage.

Meier, K. (1994). *The politics of sin: Drugs, alcohol, and public policy.* New York: M. E. Sharpe.

Meier, M. (1992). *A major malfunction: The story behind the space shuttle Challenger disaster.* Binghamton, NY: SUNY Research Foundation.

Merkle, J. A. (1980). *Management and ideology.* Berkeley: University of California Press.

Michel, J. (1979). *Dora.* London: Weidenfeld & Nicolson.

Milgram, S. (1974). *Obedience to authority.* New York: Harper and Row.

Miller, P., & O'Leary, T. (1989). Hierarchies and American ideals, 1900-1940. *Academy of Management Review, 14,* 250-265.

Morgan, D. F. (1990). Administrative phronesis: Discretion and the problem of administrative legitimacy in our constitutional system. In H. D. Kass & B. L. Catron (Eds.), *Image and identity in public administration* (pp. 67-86). Newbury Park, CA: Sage.

Mosher, F. C. (1968). *Democracy and the public service.* New York: Oxford University Press.

Murray, C. (1984). *Losing ground.* New York: Basic Books.

Nelson, M. (1982). A short ironic history of American national bureaucracy. *Journal of Politics, 44,* 747-778.

Neufeld, M. J. (1996). *The rocket and the Reich.* Cambridge, MA: Harvard University Press.

Nevitt, S., & Comstock, C. (Eds.). (1971). *Sanctions for evil.* San Francisco: Jossey-Bass.

Nietzsche, F. (1956). *The birth of tragedy and genealogy of morals* (F. Golffing, Trans.). Garden City, NY: Anchor Doubleday. (Original work published 1872)

Noble, D. F. (1958). *The paradox of progressive thought.* Minneapolis: University of Minnesota Press.

Noble, D. F. (1970). *The progressive mind, 1890-1917.* Chicago: Rand McNally.

Noble, D. F. (1977). *America by design.* New York: Alfred A. Knopf.

Nolan, M. (1994). *Visions of modernity: American business and the modernization of Germany.* New York: Oxford University Press.

Orwell, G. (1984). *Shooting an elephant and other essays.* San Diego: Harcourt, Brace, Jovanovich. (Original work published 1950)

O'Sullivan, E., & Stewart, D. W. (1984). Evaluating affirmative action programs: A case study. *Review of Public Personnel Administration, 4,* 71-82.

O'Toole, L. J., Jr. (1984). American public administration and the idea of reform. *Administration and Society, 16,* 141-166.

O'Toole, L. J., Jr. (1987). Doctrines and developments: Separation of powers, the politics-administration dichotomy, and the rise of the administrative state. *Public Administration Review, 47,* 17-25.

Parkin, D. (Ed.). (1985). *The anthropology of evil.* London: Blackwell.

Perrow, C. (1984). *Normal accidents: Living with high-risk technologies.* New York: Basic Books.

Perry, J. L., & Kraemer, K. L. (1986). Research methodology in the *Public Administration Review,* 1975-1984. *Public Administration Review, 46,* 215-226.

Phillips, S. C. (1965). *The Phillips report.* Washington, DC: National Aeronautics and Space Administration.

Piskiewicz, D. (1995). *The Nazi rocketeers: Dreams of space and crimes of war.* Westport, CT: Praeger.

Polanyi, M. (1966). *The tacit dimension.* Garden City, NY: Doubleday Anchor.

Poole, R. (1991). *Morality and modernity.* London: Routledge, Chapman and Hall.

Pugh, D. H. (1989). Professionalism in public administration. *Public Administration Review, 49,* 1-8.

Rabin, J., & Bowman, J. S. (Eds.). (1984). *Politics and administration: Woodrow Wilson and American public administration.* New York: Marcel Dekker.

Rabinbach, A. (1990). *The human motor: Energy, fatigue and the origins of modernity.* New York: Basic Books.

Redford, E. S. (1969). *Democracy in the administrative state.* New York: Oxford University Press.

Rogers, W. P. (1986). *Presidential Commission on the Space Shuttle Challenger Accident: Report.* Washington, DC: Government Printing Office.

Rohr, J. A. (1978). *Ethics for bureaucrats.* New York: Marcel Dekker.

Rohr, J. A. (1985). Professionalism legitimacy and the Constitution. *Public Administration Quarterly, 8,* 401-418.

Rohr, J. A. (1986). *To run a constitution.* Lawrence: University of Kansas Press.

Romzek, B. S., & Dubnick, M. J. (1987). Accountability in the public sector: Lessons from the *Challenger* tragedy. *Public Administration Review, 47,* 227-238.

Rosenbloom, D. H. (1971). *Federal service and the Constitution.* Ithaca, NY: Cornell University Press.

Rosenbloom, D. H. (1989). *Public administration: Understanding management, politics and law in the public sector* (2nd ed.). New York: McGraw-Hill.

Rosholt, R. L. (1966). *An administrative history of NASA, 1958-1963.* Washington, DC: Scientific and Technical Information Division, National Aeronautics and Space Administration.

Rubenstein, R. L. (1975). *The cunning of history: The Holocaust and the American future.* New York: Harper and Row.

Rubenstein, R. L. (1983). *The age of triage: Fear and hope in an overcrowded world.* Boston: Beacon.

Rubenstein, R. L. (1987). *Approaches to Auschwitz: The Holocaust and its legacy.* Atlanta: John Knox Press.

Russell, J. B. (1988). *The prince of darkness: Radical evil and the power of good in history.* Ithaca, NY: Cornell University Press.

Sanford, J. A. (1981). *Evil: The shadow side of reality.* New York: Crossroad.

Sartre, J-P. (1948). *Les Mains Sales* [Dirty Hands]. In *No exit and three other plays* (pp. 48-97). New York: Vintage.

Saul, J. R. (1992). *Voltaire's bastards: The dictatorship of reason in the West*. New York: Random House.

Schon, D. C. (1993). Generative metaphor: A perspective on problem-setting in social policy. In A. Ortony (Ed.), *Metaphor and thought* (pp. 137-163). Cambridge, UK: Cambridge University Press.

Schwartz, H. S. (1990). *Narcissistic process and corporate decay*. New York: New York University Press.

Sedgwick, J. L. (1986). Executive leadership and administration: Founding versus progressive views. *Administration and Society, 17*, 411-432.

Sedgwick, J. L. (1987). Of centennials and bicentennials: Reflections on the foundations of American public administration. *Administration and Society, 19*, 285-308.

Sereny, G. (1995). *Albert Speer: His battle with truth*. New York: Alfred A. Knopf.

Shapiro, E. R., & Carr, A. W. (1991). *Lost in familiar places: Creating new connections between the individual and society*. New Haven, CT: Yale University Press.

Simon, H. A. (1976). *Administrative behavior*. New York: Free Press.

Simpson, C. (1988). *Blowback*. New York: Weidenfeld and Nicolson.

Skowronek, S. (1982). *Building a new American state: The expansion of national administrative capacities, 1877-1920*. Cambridge, UK: Cambridge University Press.

Smith, P. (1990). *Killing the spirit: Higher education in America*. New York: Viking.

Smith, R. W. (1987). Human destruction and politics: The twentieth century as an age of genocide. In I. Walliman & M. Dobkowski (Eds.), *Genocide and the modern age: Etiology and case studies of mass death* (pp. 21-39). New York: Greenwood.

Smith, R. W. (1989). *The space telescope*. New York: Cambridge University Press.

Sofsky, W. (1997). *The order of terror: The concentration camp*. Princeton, NJ: Princeton University Press.

Speer, A. (1970). *Inside the Third Reich*. London: Weidenfeld and Nicolson.

Spragens, T. A., Jr. (1990). *Reason and democracy*. Durham, NC: Duke University Press.

Stallings, R. A., & Ferris, J. A. (1988). Public administration research: Work in *PAR*, 1940-1984. *Public Administration Review, 48*, 580-587.

Stannard, D. E. (1992). *American Holocaust: The conquest of the new world*. New York: Oxford University Press.

Staub, E. (1989). *The roots of evil: The origins of genocide and other group violence*. New York: Cambridge University Press.

Stein, H. F. (1997). Death imagery and the experience of organizational downsizing. *Administration and Society, 29*, 222-247.

Steinberg, S. (1994). *Turning back: The retreat from racial justice in American thought and policy.* Boston: Beacon.

Stever, J. A. (1986). Mary Parker Follett and the quest for pragmatic public administration. *Administration and Society, 18,* 159-177.

Stever, J. A. (1990). The dual image of the administrator in progressive administrative theory. *Administration and Society, 22,* 39-57.

Stewart, D. W. (1985a). Ethics and the profession of public administration: The moral responsibility of individuals in public sector organizations. *Public Administration Quarterly, 8,* 487-495.

Stewart, D. (1985b). Professionalism vs. democracy: Friedrich vs. Finer revisited. *Public Administration Quarterly, 9,* 13-25.

Stillman, R. J. (1987). *The American bureaucracy.* Chicago: Nelson Hall.

Stillman, R. J. (1991). *Preface to public administration: A search for themes and directions.* New York: St. Martin's.

Stivers, C. (1993). Citizenship ethics in public administration. In T. L. Cooper (Ed.), *Handbook of administrative ethics* (pp. 435-455). New York: Marcel Dekker.

Stivers, C. (1995). Settlement women and bureau men: Constructing a usable past for public administration. *Public Administration Review, 55,* 522-529.

Stivers, R. (1982). *Evil in modern myth and ritual.* Athens: University of Georgia Press.

Stone, D. A. (1988). *Policy paradox and political reason.* New York: Harper Collins.

Stuhlinger, E. F., & Ordway, F. I. (1994). *Wernher von Braun: Crusader for space.* Malabar, FL: Krieger.

Stuhlinger, E., Ordway, F., III, McCall, J., & Bucker, G. (1963). *Astronautical engineering and science from Peenemünde to planetary space.* New York: McGraw-Hill.

Sutherland, S. L. (1995). The problem of dirty hands in politics: Peace in the vegetable trade. *Canadian Journal of Political Science, 28,* 479-498.

Taylor, C. (1985). *Philosophical papers* (2 vols.). New York: Cambridge University Press.

Terry, L. D. (1995). *Leadership of public bureaucracies: The administrator as conservator.* Thousand Oaks, CA: Sage.

Thompson, D. F. (1985). The possibility of administrative ethics. *Public Administration Review, 45,* 555-561.

Trento, J. J. (1987). *Prescription for disaster: From the glory of the Apollo to the betrayal of the shuttle.* New York: Crown Publishing.

Trow, M. (1997, May 16). The chiefs of public universities should be civil servants, not political actors. *Chronicle of Higher Education,* p. A48.

Turner, B. S. (Ed.). (1990). *Theories of modernity and postmodernity.* London: Sage.

Twitchell, J. B. (1985). *Dreadful pleasures.* New York: Oxford University Press.

van Pelt, R. (1994). A site in research of a mission. In Y. Gutman & M. Berenbaum (Eds.), *Anatomy of the Auschwitz death camp* (pp. 93-156). Bloomington: University of Indiana Press.

Van Riper, P. P. (1958). *A history of the U.S. civil service.* Evanston, IL: Row, Peterson.

Van Riper, P. P. (1983). The American administrative state: Wilson and the founders—An unorthodox view. *Public Administration Review, 43,* 477-490.

Van Riper, P. P. (1990). *The Wilson influence of public administration: From theory to practice.* Washington, DC: American Society for Public Administration.

Vaughan, D. (1996). *The Challenger launch decision: Risky technology, culture, and deviance at NASA.* Chicago: University of Chicago Press.

Ventriss, C. (1993). The "publicness" of administrative ethics. In T. L. Cooper (Ed.), *Handbook of administrative ethics* (pp. 199-218). New York: Marcel Dekker.

Vickers, G. (1995). *The art of judgment.* Thousand Oaks, CA: Sage. (Original work published 1965)

Volkan, V. (1988). *The need to have enemies and allies.* Northvale, NJ: Jason Aronson.

von Braun, W. (1963). Management of the space program at a field center. In *Conference on space-age planning* (pp. 239-250). Washington, DC: National Aeronautics and Space Administration.

Waldo, D. (1948). *The administrative state: A study of the political theory of public administration.* New York: Ronald Press.

Walker, L. N. (1990). Woodrow Wilson, progressive reform and public administration. In P. P. Van Riper (Ed.), *The Wilson influence on public administration* (pp. 83-98). Washington, DC: American Society for Public Administration.

Wamsley, G. L. (1990). *Refounding public administration.* Newbury Park, CA: Sage.

Webb, J., & Liff, S. (1988). Play the white man: The social construction of fairness and competition in equal opportunity policies. *The Sociological Review, 36,* 532-551.

Weber, M. (1958). *The Protestant ethic and the spirit of capitalism.* New York: Scribners. (Original work published 1905)

Weber, M. (1979). *Economy and society* (2 vols.). Berkeley: University of California Press.

Weinstein, F. (1980). *The dynamics of Nazism: Leadership, ideology, and the Holocaust.* New York: Academic Press.

Weinstein, J. (1968). *The corporate ideal in the liberal state, 1900-1918.* Boston: Beacon.

White, J. D. (1986). On the growth of knowledge in public administration. *Public Administration Review, 46*, 15-24.

White, L. D. (1948). *The Federalists*. New York: Macmillan.

White, L. D. (1951). *The Jeffersonians*. New York: Macmillan.

White, L. D. (1954). *The Jacksonians*. New York: Macmillan.

White, L. D. (1958). *The Republican era*. New York: Macmillan.

White, M. (1957). *Social thought in America*. Boston: Beacon.

White, O. F., Jr., & McSwain, C. J. (1990). The Phoenix Project: Raising a new image of public administration from the ashes of the past. In H. D. Kass & B. L. Catron (Eds.), *Images and identities in public administration* (pp. 23-59). Newbury Park, CA: Sage.

Whitehead, A. N., & Russell, B. (1910). *Principia mathematica*. Oxford, UK: Oxford University Press.

Wiebe, R. H. (1967). *The search for order, 1877-1920*. New York: Hill and Wang.

Wilson, W. (1887). The study of administration. *Political Science Quarterly, 2*, 197-222.

Wittgenstein, L. (1922). *Tractatus logico-philosophicus*. New York: Harcourt, Brace and World.

Wyman, D. S. (1984). *The abandonment of the Jews: America and the Holocaust, 1941-1945*. New York: Pantheon.

Yahil, L. (1990). *The Holocaust: The fate of European Jewry, 1932-1945*. New York: Oxford University Press.

Yankelovich, D. (1991). *Coming to public judgment: Making democracy work in a complex world*. Syracuse, NY: Syracuse University Press.

Yanow, D. (1995). *How does a policy mean?* Washington, DC: Georgetown University Press.

Index

About the Authors

Guy B. Adams is Professor and Chair in the Department of Public Administration at the University of Missouri–Columbia. He is coeditor-in chief of the *American Review of Public Administration*. His research interests are in the areas of public administration history and theory, public service ethics, and organization studies. Adams is coauthor of *The Tacit Organization* (JAI Press, 1992) and has published more than three dozen books, book chapters, and scholarly articles in the top national public administration journals. He earned his PhD in Public Administration in 1977 from The George Washington University.

Danny L. Balfour is Associate Professor and Director of the School of Public and Nonprofit Administration at Grand Valley State University in Grand Rapids, Michigan. He is the managing editor of the *Journal of Public Affairs Education*. His research and teaching interests are in the areas of organizational theory and behavior, social policy, public service ethics, and the Holocaust. He has published more than 20 book chapters and scholarly articles in the top national public administration journals. He earned his PhD in Public Administration in 1990 from the Florida State University.